The
Phantom
Father

BARRY GIFFORD

The Phantom Father

A Memoir

CRANE HILL
PUBLISHERS

Other Books by Barry Gifford

Some of the material in this book originally appeared in *A Good Man to Know*, Clark City Press, 1992. Other material appeared, in different form, in *The Neighborhood of Baseball*, E. P. Dutton, 1981. The chapter "A Good Man to Know" received a PEN Syndicated Fiction Award and was included in *The PEN Short Story Collection*, Ballantine Books, 1985.

Published by Crane Hill Publishers
www.cranehill.com

Printed in the United States of America

Library of Congress Cataloging-in-Publication Data

Gifford, Barry, 1946-
    The phantom father : a memoir / Barry Gifford.
      p. cm.
    Originally published: New York : Harcourt, Brace & Co., 1997.
    ISBN 1-57587-178-5
    1. Gifford, Barry, 1946-   . —Homes and
haunts—Illinois—Chicago. 2. Authors, American—20th century—Family
relationships. 3. Gifford, Barry, 1946-   .—Childhood and youth. 4.
Gangsters—Illinois—Chicago—Biography. 5.
Fathers—Illinois—Chicago—Biography. 6. Chicago (Ill.)—Social life
and customs. 7. Gifford, Barry, 1946-   .—Family. 8. Winston,
Rudy.   I. Title.
    PS3557.I283 Z47 2001
    813'.54—dc21

                                        2001047006

10   9   8   7   6   5   4   3   2   1

For Mark

*and in homage to Nelson Algren,
who wrote, "the Chicago of the
nineteen-forties is unrecorded
and that of the fifties
is sunk for keeps."*

Contents

Author's Note

The Japanese form *shōsetsu* is defined by the eminent translator (*The Tale of Genji, The Makioka Sisters,* etc.) Edward Seidensticker as "a piece of autobiography or a set of memoirs, somewhat embroidered and colored but essentially nonfiction." Yasunari Kawabata considered his "faithful chronicle-novel" *The Master of Go* to be in the realm of *shōsetsu.* As Mr. Seidensticker has noted, while *shōsetsu* contains elements of fiction, it is "a rather more flexible and generous and catholic term than 'novel.' " *The Phantom Father* belongs to the genre of *shōsetsu* and should be approached as such by the reader.

—B.G.

*The father, dead very early . . .
merely touched the surface of childhood
with an almost silent bounty.*
—*ROLAND BARTHES*

*When I met [Meyer Lansky
and Doc Stacher] by chance in
the lobby of the Tel Aviv Sheraton . . .
I was caused to blurt: 'Gentlemen, it's like
meeting Ruth and Gehrig.'*
—*SIDNEY ZION*

Foreword

In November 1993 I traveled to Vienna, Austria, and with the help of my friend Daniel Schmid discovered the address of the house where my father lived as a child, 5 Zirkusgasse, in the area named Leopoldstadt. This was accomplished by searching through the residential directory of the year 1917, one year prior to my father's family's departure for the United States, when he was eight years old. The residential documents pertaining to my grandfather show that the family had come to Vienna from the Bukovina, a mysterious region of the eastern Carpathian Mountains, which at that time was part of the Austro-Hungarian empire belonging to Austria. Following World War I the region passed into the hands of Romania, and after World War II it was incorporated with Bessarabia and became part of the Soviet state of Ukraine, currently an independent republic.

The Bukovina was a thickly forested area, populated by people who spoke High German and carried on what the writer Gregor von Rezzori, who was born there, referred to as the last of the Old German ways. Located at a point where Austria then joined Transylvania and Moldavia, The Bukovina was also home to a rather Bohemian collection of *ausländers*, outsiders comprised of Gypsies, Jews, and other nomadic types. My family came not from the main city, Cernowitz, where von Rezzori's people resided, but a rural section near the Borgo Pass, close to where Vlad Tepic—known as the Impaler, upon whose exploits the legend of Dracula came to be based—had his castle.

I do not know whether my father was born in the Bukovina or in Vienna. The house in which the family lived in Vienna on Zirkusgasse was torn down in the early 1970s and replaced by an institutionally plain apartment building. Oddly enough, Daniel Schmid's longtime friend Cornelia Wonder, who still lives in Vienna and was of great assistance to us in cutting through the red tape at city hall, had lived at that very address, number 5 Zirkusgasse, when she first came to Vienna from rural Austria twenty years before.

When my father's family left Vienna in 1918, immediately after the cessation of World War I, they stated on their departure application the intended destination of Bukovina, Romania. Most probably this was the only place to which they could receive permission to emigrate, since it was where they had come from originally. Instead of going to what was now part of a country to which they had no allegiance—and that was no doubt in an even more economically depressed condition than Vienna—they faked left and went right, to America. Within the year they had settled in Chicago.

BUCOVINA {boo-koh-vee'-nuh}

Bucovina (or Bukovina) is a region in the northeastern Carpathian Mountains of east central Europe that is now shared by Romania and Ukraine. The area is heavily wooded, and the Carpathians serve as the source of the Prut, Dnestr, and Siret Rivers, which flow to the Black Sea. Bucovina covers an area of 8,796 square kilometers (3,396 square miles). The climate is moderate, with temperatures ranging from –7 degrees Celsius (20 degrees Fahrenheit) to 29 degrees Celsius (85 degrees Fahrenheit) annually. Forest products, iron ore, and grains are the area's main output. The inhabitants are a mix of Ukrainians, Russians, and Romanians. The main Ukrainian city is Chernovtsy; Romanian cities include Suceava and Botosani.

Historically a part of the Moldavian principality, Bucovina was ruled by Austria from 1775 to 1918 and became a separate crown land in 1849. From 1918 to 1940 it was part of Romania; then the USSR annexed it and incorporated it with Bessarabia. It was reshaped in 1947, with the southern half becoming part of northern Romania and the northern half part of the Ukrainian SSR (since 1991 independent Ukraine).

The Morgue

Rudy Winston, Popular Rush Street Figure, Dies

Anybody who knows anything about what goes on in the city of Chicago knows that for the past twenty-five years much of that activity has taken place in and around the Lake Shore Liquor Store on the corner of Chicago and Rush Streets. Now that Rudy Winston, the proprietor of Lake Shore Liquors, is dead, things are bound to be different. Rudy Winston's colorful circle of friends and acquaintances encompassed virtually every person of importance to live in or pass through Chicago during the past two and a half decades.

Politicians, movie stars, high rollers, low rollers, no rollers, thieves, murderers, showgirls, junkies, bums, newspapermen, and every cop in the city knew or knew of Rudy Winston. If you were out of pocket, and were an OK Joe, Rudy was good for ten. If you needed a place to go for a while where nobody would find you, Rudy found you a place. Needed some publicity? Rudy made a call and the next day your name was in the gossips. He was on a first-name basis with the mayor, the governor, the Cardinal, the Capones.

Who was this guy, anyway, you ask? If you never got the chance to know Rudy Winston, all I can say is, I'm sorry. He was one of the guys who made this city go, and now he's gone too young. It's a shame, because Rudy Winston was a good man to know.

Obituary in
the *Chicago Sun-Times*
December 5, 1958

WINSTON—Rudolph Aaron Winston of 6441 N. Ravenswood Avenue, dearly beloved husband of Eva; devoted father of James Barry and William Irwin; loving son of Ezra and the late Aura; dear brother of Bruno M. Winston and Irma Fox. Service Friday, 1 P.M., at chapel, 4300 W. Peterson Avenue. Interment Westlawn Cemetery. Member of Chicago Retail Liquor Association. Inf. Rogers Park 4-1150.

Obituary in
the *Chicago Tribune*
December 5, 1958

Rudolph A. Winston, 47, of 6441 N. Ravenswood Avenue, owner since 1932 of the Lake Shore Liquor Store at 101 E. Chicago Avenue, died Thursday in Columbus Memorial Hospital. He was graduated from the University of Illinois in 1932 and was well known in Chicago for his participation in civic and charitable affairs. Survivors include his widow, Eva; two sons, James and William Winston; and his father, Ezra.

Bandits Slug, Rob Man on North Side

CHICAGO, July 3, 1943— Rudy Winston, cafe-society luminary, was robbed and assaulted yesterday by two strong-arm bandits, the police reported today.

Winston had just left the Rio Cabana, Near North Side night spot, when the bandits forced their way into Winston's Cadillac sedan as it stopped for a traffic light at Michigan Avenue and Delaware Place. Winston attempted to resist and was beaten around the head and face. Then the bandits ordered Winston to drive on. At 2640 Dayton St. Winston was relieved of $175. He was taken to Illinois Masonic Hospital where his injuries required four stitches.

Winston gained notoriety for a fracas earlier this year when he felled Milwaukee Ace brewery owner Edward Danillo with a right hook in the foyer of the Ambassador Hotel. Danillo refused to press charges and paid the hotel for damage caused to a plate-glass window.

John Dillinger Aide Begins 1 to 10 Years in Prison

CHICAGO, Dec. 14, 1945—Samuel "Dummy" Fish, 42, said to have been a contact man for the gang headed by the late John Dillinger, was taken to Stateville prison yesterday to begin serving a 1- to 10-year term imposed in Criminal Court Nov. 26, 1942, upon his conviction on a charge of receiving stolen property. He was convicted of receiving $3,000 worth of stolen furs.

Rudolf A. Winston, of Chicago, arrested with Fish, was convicted as being an accessory to the crime and given a suspended sentence of 1 year.

Willie "the Hero" Wins Release As Suspect in Vault Robbery

CHICAGO, April 17, 1946—Willie "the Hero" Nero, former Capone hoodlum, was plucked from the Lake Shore Liquor Store at the corner of Chicago and Rush Streets yesterday by a police squad and hustled to the Criminal Courts Building to be questioned about a $2,000,000 robbery, but he sauntered out a short time later, a free man because police admitted they had no evidence to warrant holding him.

Nero told Blair Varnes, assistant State's attorney, that he knew nothing about the Jan. 20 looting of the vault of the E. H. Rumboldt Real Estate Co., 624 W. 119th St. Before the grand jury he stood on his constitutional rights and refused to answer questions.

"I am a businessman," Nero told reporters after being released. "I own a bowling alley. I never robbed anybody."

Find Body in Car on West Side

CHICAGO, July 13, 1946— Gangland guns barked death here again today in what police called a burst of violence in the liquor black market.

The victim was Arnold "Suitcase Solly" Banks, 30, of 1300 Marine Drive, whiskey salesman and suspected operator in a liquor black market flourishing between Chicago and New York.

He was shot to death in an auto in front of 1622 Ontario Street during the night in a fashion reminiscent of Prohibition-day liquors wars. Banks's body, a bullet hole in his head, was found behind the wheel of his 1942 maroon Mercury sedan at 6:40 A.M. The motor was still running and the radiator was boiling.

Deputy Chief of Detectives Arthur Grant said: "There is a general belief that Banks was slain because others thought he had squealed, or was getting ready to squeal, about the black market."

Banks's pockets had been emptied of everything, and his wristwatch was missing. Three quarters lay on the seat, all that remained of the $1,000 he had collected earlier from Rudolph A. Winston, the proprietor of Lake Shore Liquor Store, Rush Street.

The victim's wife, Arlene, 26, former professional dancer at Colosimo's and other nightclubs, became hysterical when she learned of the killing. She refused to view the body.

"Suitcase Solly" went into the liquor business in 1941 as a salesman for the Blue Seal Liquor Co., a business, police said, owned and operated by Capone mob big shot Willie "the Hero" Nero. Nero is known to have been a beer boss during Prohibition days.

Banks is reputed to have gained his nickname of "Suitcase Solly" due to his having carried large amounts of cash from one location to another for the mob.

On Dec. 1, 1943, Banks was indicted with Maurice Goldberg, owner of the Spotless Distribution Co., 30 E. 88th St.; Pete Licavoli, a big figure in the Detroit rackets; George Prieto, another Detroit gangster; and Rudolph A. Winston, for distributing hijacked liquor. No convictions were obtained.

Poet Suspect in Murder of Former Showgirl

CHICAGO, Dec, 16, 1955—Charles Wodarski, 27, of 32 S. Halsted St., a blond, blue-eyed poet and former employee of the Lake Shore Liquor Store, was seized by police yesterday for questioning in the investigation of the "lipstick murder" of Miss Diane Wood, 38, attractive former showgirl at the Club Alabam, Rush Street. Miss Wood was found shot and stabbed last Monday in her apartment in the Pine View Hotel.

The suspect was arrested at his home on an anonymous tip. Wodarski, who wears his hair unusually long, gave his occupation as a dishwasher. His pockets were filled with poetry, written on restaurant menu cards.

The poetry and other clues to Wodarski's handwriting were given to the police crime detection laboratory for comparison with the writing that was found in lipstick on a wall in Miss Wood's room.

The suspect was asked by police to write the words on the wall: "For heaven's sake, stop me before I kill more."

As he complied, Wodarski said: "So that's what you want me for, to ask about the murder of the woman."

A Good Man
to Know

A Good Man to Know

I was seven years old in June of 1954 when my dad and I drove from Miami to New Orleans to visit his friend Albert Thibodeaux. It was a cloudy, humid morning when we rolled into town in my dad's powder blue Cadillac. The river smell mixed with malt from the Jax brewery and the smoke from my dad's chain of Lucky Strikes to give the air an odor of toasted heat. We parked the car by Jackson Square and walked over a block to Tujague's bar to meet Albert. "It feels like it's going to rain," I said to Dad. "It always feels like this in New Orleans," he said.

Albert Thibodeaux was a gambler. In the evenings he presided over cockfight and pit-bull matches across the river in Gretna or Algiers but during the day he hung out at Tujague's on Decatur Street with the railroad men and phony artists from the Quarter. He and my dad knew each other from the old days in Cuba, which I knew nothing about except that they'd both lived at the Nacional in Havana.

According to Nanny, my mother's mother, my dad didn't even speak to me until I was five years old. He apparently didn't consider a child capable of understanding him or a friendship worth cultivating until that age and he may have been correct in his judgment. I certainly never felt deprived as a result of this policy. If my grandmother hadn't told me about it I would have never known the difference.

My dad never really told me about what he did or had done before I was old enough to go around with him. I picked up information as I went, listening to guys like Albert and some of my dad's other friends like Willie Nero in Chicago and Dummy Fish in New York. We supposedly lived in Chicago but my dad had places in Miami, New York, and Acapulco. We traveled, mostly without my mother, who stayed at the house in Chicago and went to church a lot. Once I asked my dad if we were any particular religion and he said, "Your mother's a Catholic."

Albert was a short, fat man with a handlebar mustache. He looked like a Maxwell Street organ-grinder without the organ or the monkey. He and my dad drank Irish whiskey from ten in the morning until lunchtime, which was around one-thirty, when they sent me down to the Central Grocery on Decatur or to Johnny's on St. Louis Street for muffalettas. I brought back three of them but Albert and Dad didn't eat theirs. They just talked and once in a while Albert went into the back to make a phone call. They got along just fine and about once an hour Albert would ask if I wanted something, like a Barq's or a Delaware Punch, and Dad would rub my shoulder and say to Albert, "He's a real piece of meat, this boy." Then Albert would grin so that his mustache covered the front of his nose and say, "He is, Rudy. You won't want to worry about him."

When Dad and I were in New York one night I heard him talking in a loud voice to Dummy Fish in the lobby of the Waldorf. I was sitting in a big leather chair between a sand-filled ashtray and a potted palm and Dad came over and told me that Dummy would take me upstairs to our room. I should go to sleep, he said, he'd be back late. In the elevator I looked at Dummy and saw that he was sweating. It was December but water ran down from his temples to his chin. "Does my dad have a job?" I asked Dummy. "Sure he does," he said. "Of course. Your dad has to work, just like everybody else." "What is it?" I asked. Dummy wiped the sweat from his face with a white-and-blue checkered handkerchief. "He talks to people," Dummy told me. "Your dad is a great talker."

Dad and Albert talked right past lunchtime and I must have fallen asleep on the bar because when I woke up it was dark out and I was in the backseat of the car. We were driving across the Huey P. Long Bridge and a freight train was running along the tracks over our heads. "How about some Italian oysters, son?" my dad asked. "We'll stop up here in Houma and get some cold beer and dinner." We were cruising in the passing lane in the powder blue Caddy over the big brown river. Through the bridge railings I watched the barge lights twinkle as they inched ahead through the water.

"Albert's a businessman, the best kind." Dad lit a fresh Lucky from an old one and threw the butt out the window. "He's a good man to know, remember that."

The Old Country

My grandfather never wore an overcoat. That was Ezra, my father's father, who had a candy stand under the Addison Street elevated tracks near Wrigley Field. Even in winter, when it was ten below and the wind cut through the station, Ezra never wore more than a heavy sport coat, and sometimes, when Aunt Belle, his second wife, insisted, a woolen scarf wrapped up around his chin. He was six foot two and two hundred pounds, had his upper lip covered by a bushy mustache, and a full head of dark hair until he died at ninety, not missing a day at his stand till six months before.

He never told anyone his business. He ran numbers from the stand and owned an apartment building on the South Side. He outlived three wives and one of his sons, my father. His older son, my uncle Bruno, looked just like him, but Bruno was mean and defensive whereas Ezra was brusque but kind. He always gave me and my friends gum or candy on our way to and from the ballpark, and he liked me to hang around there or at another stand he had for a while at Belmont Avenue, especially on Saturdays so he could show me off to his regular cronies. He'd put me on a box behind the stand and keep one big hand on my shoulder. "This is my *grandson*," he'd say, and wait until he was sure they had looked at me. I was the first and then his only grandson; Uncle Bruno had two girls. "Good *boy!*"

He left it to his sons to make the big money, and they did all right, my dad with the rackets and the liquor store, Uncle Bruno as an auctioneer, but they never had to take care of the old man, he took care of himself.

Ezra spoke broken English; he came to America with his sons (my dad was eight, Bruno fourteen) and a daughter from Vienna in 1918. I always remember him standing under the tracks outside the station in February, cigar stub poked out between mustache and muffler, waiting for me and my dad to pick him up. When we'd pull up along the curb my dad would honk but the old man wouldn't notice. I would always have to run out and get him. I figured Ezra always saw us but waited for me to come for him. It made him feel better if I got out and grabbed his hand and led him to the car.

"Pa, for Chrissakes, why don't you wear an overcoat?" my dad would ask. "It's cold."

The old man wouldn't look over or answer right away. He'd sit with me on his lap as my father pointed the car into the dark.

"What cold?" he'd say after we'd gone a block or two. "In the *old* country was cold."

Nanny

From the time I was four until I was eight my grandmother lived with us. She slept in the big bedroom with my mother (my father had remarried by then) and was bedridden most of the time, her heart condition critical, killing her just past her sixtieth birthday. I called her Nanny, for no reason I can remember, and I loved her, as small boys suppose they do. My mother was often away in those days, and while I don't remember Nanny ever feeding me (too sick to get out of bed for that) or dressing me, or making me laugh (there was Flo for that, my black mammy who later "ran off with some man," as my mother was wont to disclose; and then a succession of other maids and nurses most of whom, again according to my mother, either ransacked liquor cabinets or ran away à la Flo—anyone who left my mother always "ran off"), I do remember her scolding me, and once my mother was in Puerto Rico, for some reason I'm sure Nanny considered adequate (sufficient to pry her from bed), she backed me into a corner of my room against the full-length mirror on my closet door (thus I watched her though my back was turned) and beat me with a board, me screaming, "My mother'll get you for this!"; and when my mother returned my not believing it was really her (she being so brown from the sun), and my momentary fear of her being an impostor, some woman hired by my grandmother to beat me because it was too hard on her heart for her to do it herself.

This repeated paranoia, persistent tension, allowed no relief for me then but through my toy soldiers, sworded dragoons, Zouaves, and Vikings that I manipulated, controlled. Hours alone on my lined linoleum floor I played, determinedly oblivious to the voices, agonies perpetuated dining room to kitchen to bedroom.

And there was the race we never ran. Nanny and I planned a race for when she was well, though she never would be. Days sick I'd sit in my mother's bed next to Nanny and devise the route, from backyard down the block to the corner, from the fence to the lamppost and back—and Nanny would nod, "Yes, certainly, soon as I'm well"—and I'd cut out comics or draw, listening to Sergeant Preston on the radio, running the race in my mind, running it over and over, never once seeing Nanny run with me.

The Monster

I used to sit on a stool at the counter of the soda fountain in my dad's drugstore and talk to Louise, the counter waitress, while she made milk shakes and grilled cheese sandwiches. I especially liked to be there on Saturday mornings when the organ-grinder came in with his monkey. The monkey and I would dunk doughnuts together in the organ-grinder's coffee. The regular customers would always stop and say something to me, and tell my dad how much I looked like him, only handsomer.

One Saturday morning when I was about six, while I was waiting for the organ-grinder and his monkey to come in, I started talking to Louise about scary movies. I had seen *Frankenstein* the night before and I told Louise it was the scariest movie I'd ever seen, even scarier than *The Beast from 20,000 Fathoms* that my dad had taken me to see at the Oriental Theater when I was five. I had had dreams about the beast ripping up Coney Island and dropping big blobs of blood all over the streets ever since, but the part where the Frankenstein monster kills the little girl while she's picking flowers was worse than that.

"The scariest for me," Louise told me, "is *Dracula*. There'll never be another one like that."

I hadn't seen *Dracula* and I asked her what it was about. Louise put on a new pot of coffee, then she turned and rested her arms on the counter in front of me.

"Sex, honey," she said. "Dracula was a vampire who went around attacking women. Oh, he might have attacked a man now and then, but he mainly went after the girls. Scared me to death when I saw it. I can't watch it now. I remember his eyes."

Then Louise went to take care of a customer. I stared at myself in the mirror behind the counter and thought about the little girl picking flowers with the monster.

Sunday Paper

As he often did when I was about eight or nine and he still lived with us, Pops, my mother's father, asked me to go for the Sunday paper. For some reason on this particular day I decided to go to the stand on Washtenaw instead of the one on Rockwell, taking the shortcut through the alley where the deep snow from the night before was still undisturbed, no cars having gone over it yet that morning. I was shuffling through the powder, kicking it up in the air so that the flakes floated about in the sunlight like rice snow in crystal balls, when I spotted the police cars.

There were three of them, parked one behind the other on Washtenaw in front of Talon's Butcher Shop. A few people stood bundled in coats outside Talon's, trying to see inside the shop, which I knew was closed on Sunday. I stood on the opposite side of the street and watched. An ambulance came, without using its siren, and slid slowly to a stop alongside the police cars. Two attendants got out and went into Talon's carrying a stretcher.

A man came up beside me and asked what was going on. I looked at him and saw that he had on an overcoat over his pajamas and probably slippers on under his galoshes.

"I was just going for a paper," he said.

When I told him I didn't know, he crossed over and spoke to one of the women standing by the door of the butcher shop. The man looked in the doorway and then walked away. I waited, standing in a warm shaft of sunlight, and in a couple of minutes the man came up to me again. He had a rolled-up *Tribune* under his arm.

"He hanged himself," the man said. "Talon, the butcher. They found him hanging in his shop this morning."

The man looked across the street for a moment, then walked down Washtenaw.

Nobody came out of the butcher shop. I went to the corner and bought a *Sun-Times*. I stopped for a few seconds on my way back to see if anything was happening but nothing was so I turned into the alley, carefully stepping in the tracks I'd made before.

Mrs. Kashfi

My mother has always been a great believer in fortune-tellers, a predilection my dad considered as bizarre as her devotion to the Catholic Church. He refused even to discuss anything having to do with either entity, a policy that seemed only to reinforce my mother's arcane quest. Even now she informs me whenever she's stumbled upon a seer whose prognostications strike her as being particularly apt. I once heard my dad describe her as belonging to "the sisterhood of the Perpetual Pursuit of the Good Word."

My own experience with fortune-tellers is limited to what I observed as a small boy, when I had no choice but to accompany my mother on her frequent pilgrimages to Mrs. Kashfi. Mrs. Kashfi was a tea-leaf reader who lived with her bird in a two-room apartment in a large gray brick building on Hollywood Avenue in Chicago. As soon as we entered the downstairs lobby the stuffiness of the place began to overwhelm me. It was as if Mrs. Kashfi lived in a vault to which no fresh air was admitted. The lobby, elevator, and hallways were suffocating, too hot both in summer, when there was too little ventilation, and in winter, when the building was unbearably overheated. And the whole place stank terribly, as if no food other than boiled cabbage were allowed to be prepared. My mother, who was usually all too aware of these sorts of unappealing aspects, seemed blissfully unaware of them at Mrs. Kashfi's. The oracle was in residence, and that was all that mattered.

The worst olfactory assault, however, came from Mrs. Kashfi's apartment, in the front room where her bird, a blind, practically featherless dinge-yellow parakeet, was kept and whose cage Mrs. Kashfi failed to clean with any regularity. It was in that room, on a lumpy couch with dirt-gray lace doily arm covers, that I was made to wait for my mother while she and Mrs. Kashfi, locked in the inner sanctum of the bedroom, voyaged into the sea of clairvoyance.

The apartment was filled with overstuffed chairs and couches, dressers crowded with bric-a-brac and framed photographs of strangely dressed, stiff and staring figures, relics of the old country, which to me appeared as evidence of extraterrestrial existence. Nothing seemed quite real, as if with a snap of Mrs. Kashfi's sorceress's fingers the entire scene would disappear. Mrs. Kashfi herself was a small, very old woman who was permanently bent slightly forwards so that she appeared about to topple over, causing me to avoid allowing her to hover over me for longer than a moment. She had a large nose and she wore glasses, as well as two or more dark green or brown sweaters at all times, despite the already hellish climate.

I dutifully sat on the couch, listening to the murmurings from beyond the bedroom door, and to the blind bird drop pelletlike feces onto the stained newspaper in its filthy cage. No sound issued from the parakeet's enclosure other than the constant "tup, tup" of its evacuation. Behind the birdcage was a weather-smeared window, covered with eyelet curtains, that looked out on the brick wall of another building.

I stayed put on the couch and waited for my mother's session to end. Each visit lasted about a half hour, at the finish of which Mrs. Kashfi would walk my mother to the doorway, where they'd stand and talk for another ten minutes while I fidgeted in the smelly hall trying to see how long I could hold my breath.

Only once did I have a glimpse of the mundane evidence from which Mrs. Kashfi made her miraculous analysis. At the conclusion of a session my mother came out of the bedroom carrying a teacup, which she told me to look into.

"What does it mean?" I asked.

"Your grandmother is safe and happy," my mother said.

My grandmother, my mother's mother, had recently died, so this news puzzled me. I looked again at the brown bits in the bottom of the china cup. Mrs. Kashfi came over and leaned above me, nodding her big nose with long hairs in the nostrils. I moved away and waited by the door, wondering what my dad would have thought of all this, while my mother stood smiling, staring into the cup.

Tecumseh,
the Greatest Indian

When I was four and a half years old I was sent to camp in Eagle River, Wisconsin, several hours by train north of Chicago. I was by two and a half years the youngest boy at the camp, which season lasted two months, July and August. The campers slept in cabins arranged according to age. I went to the camp for three years (in 1951, '53, and '54) and was always resident in the youngest side of the youngest cabin, called Frontier Lodge.

The name of the camp was Tecumseh Lodge. A small log house, supposedly used by the Shawnee Indian Tecumseh when he was on a campaign to unite the tribes of the Old Northwest—Sauk and Fox, Winnebago, Menominee—was within the camp boundary. Tecumseh had been a great man, we were told at the camp, even though he was an Indian.

My main activity at Tecumseh was trail riding. Each of the riders was given a horse to take care of. The first year I had a calico named Chico, an easygoing older horse. Since I was so young, and could mount Chico only by standing on a box or being lifted aboard, the riding master, Cy Sullivan, didn't expect too much of me. I was a pretty good horseman for four and a half years old, though, the only really unfortunate incident occurring when once I lagged behind the group and kicked Chico to catch up. I was jolted off by his sudden start and rolled down an incline into a clump of bushes. It frightened me, I was a little banged up and refused to get back on Chico, so Cy Sullivan had to put me up on his horse, Pepper, with him.

The second and third years I had a horse named Moonlight, a wilder black horse with a patch of white on his forehead. I never fell off Moonlight, but he was harder to handle than Chico. Some of the older boys had gentler horses, and I was proud that Cy had such confidence in me.

In fact, one night when the horses broke out of the corral Cy enlisted me in the roundup party. It took until dawn to collect them. It was beautiful to see the horses running loose like that. I was with one of the counselors, Warren Eagle, an Ojibway Indian, who did the roping and bridling. I rode the horse bareback back to the corral.

By my third year at Tecumseh I was old enough—I skipped the year after my first year because the camp owner thought it best that I "mature" some, as he told my parents, before returning—even though I was still the smallest kid in camp (it was easy for me to find my place in line at morning reveille—since we lined up according to height, I was always the first!), to attend the occasional "socials" with the neighboring girls' camp, Jack O'Lantern. These dances were always scheduled on Saturday nights, which was when the Nighthawks, the elite trail-riding group of which I was a member, went on special pathfinding patrols. We were supposed to individually follow a subtly marked trail blazed by Cy Sullivan and were graded according to the time it took to complete the ride. Some of the trails were extremely difficult to follow, and Cy often had to go out after lost riders.

So I would usually swagger late into the dance dressed in my dusty trail jeans and boots, feeling lean and wiry and tough compared to the other boys who'd put on BanLon shirts and slacks and had their hair combed neat. Even though I wasn't quite eight years old I could play the role, lean against a post chewing gum and casually look over the girls on the dance floor. The boys who'd been on the trail ride tried to appear as aloof as possible. After all, we were the Nighthawks, cowboys, and wanted to make sure everyone knew we were special.

I was afraid of the girls, though. All during the time on the trail I couldn't help but think about the dance later, and what I could say to the girls. Most of the time I didn't dance, just stood around and watched, drank bug juice, and tried not to look anybody in the eye.

But once in a while I'd spot a girl I really liked the looks of and ask her to dance. The few times I did this the girls turned out to be a year or so older than me. I told them some ridiculous stories, about how I'd been raised in the desert in Mexico by bandits and used to kill snakes with my pocketknife, then skin and eat them, crazy stories. I didn't really care whether or not they believed me, I just liked to tell the stories. I never knew what I was going to say, and even then the nicest audience I could imagine was a pretty girl who didn't quite know what to make of me.

Life in Frontier Lodge wasn't so good. Most of the counselors were insensitive to the kids, didn't care about them. When it came time to pack the campers' trunks at the end of the summer they'd throw anybody's stuff anywhere. I always wound up back home with three pairs of gym shoes that weren't mine, no underwear, one pair of pants, thirty T-shirts, and everyone else's socks.

One year my dad sent me up a case of my favorite Whiz and Tango candy bars, which I put under my, or really my bunkmate's, bunk, since I slept on top. My bunkmate was a bed wetter, though, and the first night he peed right through the mattress and the thin cardboard cover of the box of candy bars and ruined them.

Bed wetters had a tough time. Every morning you could see them, like lepers in India, dragging their sheets and mattresses out the back doors of the lodges to dry in the sun while the counselors kept their distance and told them to hurry up.

The single great event of the summer was the Green and White War. Those were the camp colors. Half of the boys wore green T-shirts with the head of an Indian in a war bonnet outlined in white, and the other half wore white T-shirts with the head of an Indian in a war bonnet outlined in green, both emblazoned with the words TECUMSEH LODGE across the top.

The war was a series of track-and-field events. I always ran the short sprints, forty, fifty, and sixty yards, and one leg of the final event, the cross-country race. My third and last year at Tecumseh I came in second in all three sprints to a kid from Milwaukee named Barney Kaminski. In previous years I had always won at least one or two of those races, but Kaminski was too fast for me— he was older by about six months, and much bigger—even so he only beat me by a couple of steps each time. Going into the last race, the White team was ahead of the Green by a small margin. My team could still win the war if we beat the White in the cross-country.

I was scheduled to run the next-to-last lap, but one of my team, the kid who was supposed to run the first lap, wasn't feeling well and couldn't run. Warren Eagle, who was our coach that year, told me to run the first lap instead, but I wanted to run the penultimate lap: it was the longest and most important part of the race, and Kaminski was going to run the final leg for the Whites. I wanted to make sure my team had a big enough lead so that Kaminski couldn't possibly pull it out.

Warren said that I could run both laps but it meant that after I'd completed the first lap I'd have to run a half mile across the grounds to be in position for the other lap. Warren was afraid I would be too tired, but I told him I could do it, there'd be enough time to rest if I just kept on running after the first stretch. I could sit on the hill above the camp for a half hour while I waited for the runner to get there.

I won the first lap, but only by a little, and immediately after handing off the baton I cut across to the hill on the edge of the grounds. It was a brutally hot late August after-noon, and by the time I got there I was exhausted. I lay down on the hill panting and sweating. The White team runner was loosening up, stretching and touching his toes. The thirty minutes went by much too quickly. When I saw the White team runner line up in position I jumped up and took a look: the Green and White midstretch men were dead even. I took my place, and the White runner and I took the batons together.

Halfway down the hill the White runner had a step on me but then he fell. He got right up again but I was several yards ahead. My side hurt but I didn't want to lose the lead, it was just what our team needed to beat Kaminski. By the time we reached the tennis courts, in full view of the other campers, who were yelling and screaming, the White runner had made up more than half of the difference between us.

Poised on the far side of the courts was Kaminski, wearing a white headband around his curly blond hair, leaning away, right hand held back to take the white baton.

I wasn't going to have enough of a lead to beat him. I handed off my baton three steps ahead of the White team and kept running—I wanted to see what happened. Kaminski was catching up but our anchor man hung on until the last ten yards, where Kaminski passed him and won the race.

The White team mobbed Kaminski. I sat down on the steps of the recreation hall and tried to catch my breath. Warren Eagle came over and sat next to me. He didn't say anything. He really looked like an Indian: his skin was dark, his hair was black, his nose sloped. He always wore a plain white T-shirt, khaki pants with a red-and-blue beaded belt that said EAGLE RIVER on it, and white socks with unpolished ROTC shoes. We sat there and watched the White team jump around and slap each other on the back.

"You disappointed?" he asked.

I shrugged my shoulders. I was breathing evenly again.

"You coming back next year?"

"I don't know," I said. "Are you?"

"I'm going into the army. I'll probably be in Korea."

"The Cubs beat Brooklyn yesterday," said Warren.

"Who pitched?"

"Rush."

"Think he'll win twenty?"

"No, but he would if he were with Brooklyn."

The dinner-warning gong rang.

"Watermelon for dessert tonight."

"I don't like watermelon," I said. "I used to, but it makes me nauseated."

We stood up and Warren shook my hand.

"You did all right," he said. "Good luck to you."

"Thanks," I said, and ran off to wash up.

An Eye on the Alligators

I knew as the boat pulled in to the dock there were no alligators out there. I got up and stuck my foot against the piling so that it wouldn't scrape the boat, then got out and secured the bowline to the nearest cleat. Mr. Reed was standing on the dock now, helping my mother up out of the boat. Her brown legs came up off the edge weakly, so that Mr. Reed had to lift her to keep her from falling back. The water by the pier was blue black and stank of oil and gas, not like out on the ocean, or in the channel, where we had been that day.

Mr. Reed had told me to watch for the alligators. The best spot to do it from, he said, was up on the bow. So I crawled up through the trapdoor on the bow and watched for the alligators. The river water was clear and green.

"Look around the rocks," Mr. Reed shouted over the engine noise, "the gators like the rocks." So I kept my eye on the rocks, but there were no alligators.

"I don't see any," I shouted. "Maybe we're going too fast and the noise scares them away."

After that Mr. Reed went slower but still there were no alligators. We were out for nearly three hours and I didn't see one.

"It was just a bad day for seeing alligators, son," said Mr. Reed. "Probably because of the rain. They don't like to come up when it's raining."

For some reason I didn't like it when Mr. Reed called me "son." I wasn't his son. Mr. Reed, my mother told me, was a friend of my father's. My dad was not in Florida with us, he was in Chicago doing business while my mother and I rode around in boats and visited alligator farms.

Mr. Reed had one arm around me and one arm around my mother.

"Can we go back tomorrow?" I asked.

My mother laughed. "That's up to Mr. Reed," she said. "We don't want to impose on him too much."

"Sure kid," said Mr. Reed. Then he laughed, too.

I looked up at Mr. Reed, then out at the water. I could see the drops disappearing into their holes on the surface.

The Mason-Dixon Line

One Sunday I accompanied my dad on an automobile trip up from Chicago to Dixon, Illinois. It was a sunny January morning, and it must have been when I was ten years old because I remember that I wore the black leather motorcycle jacket I'd received that Christmas. I was very fond of that jacket with its multitude of bright silver zippers and two silver stars on each epaulet. I also wore a blue cashmere scarf of my dad's and an old pair of brown leather gloves he'd given me after my mother gave him a new pair of calfskins for Christmas.

I liked watching the snowy fields as we sped past them on the narrow, two-lane northern Illinois roads. We passed through a number of little towns, each of them with seemingly identical centers: a Rexall, hardware store, First State Bank of Illinois, Presbyterian, Methodist, and Catholic churches with snowcapped steeples, and a statue of Black Hawk, the heroic Sauk and Fox chief.

When my dad had asked me if I wanted to take a ride with him that morning I'd said sure, without asking where to or why. My dad never asked twice and he never made any promises about when we'd be back. I liked the uncertainty of those situations, the open-endedness about them. Anything could happen, I figured; it was more fun not knowing what to expect.

"We're going to Dixon," Dad said after we'd been driving for about forty-five minutes. "To see a man named Mason." I'd recently read a Young Readers biography of Robert E. Lee, so I knew all about the Civil War. "We're on the Mason-Dixon line," I said, and laughed, pleased with my little kid's idea of a joke. "That's it, boy," said my dad. "We're going to get a line on Mason in Dixon."

The town of Dixon appeared to be one street long, like in a Western movie: the hardware store, bank, church, and drugstore. I didn't see a statue. We went into a tiny cafe next to the bank that was empty except for a counterman. Dad told me to sit in one of the booths and told the counterman to give me a hot chocolate and whatever else I wanted.

"I'll be back in an hour, son," said Dad. He gave the counterman a twenty-dollar bill and walked out. When the counterman brought over the hot chocolate he asked if there was anything else he could get for me. "A hamburger," I said, "and an order of fries." "You got it," he said.

I sipped slowly at the hot chocolate until he brought me the hamburger and fries. The counterman sat on a stool near the booth and looked at me. "That your old man?" he asked. "He's my dad," I said, between bites of the hamburger. "Any special reason he's here?" he asked. I didn't say anything and the counterman said, "You are from Chi, aren't ya?" I nodded yes and kept chewing. "You must be here for a reason," he said. "My dad needs to see someone," I said. "Thought so," said the counterman. "Know his name?" I took a big bite of the hamburger before I answered. "No," I said. The counterman looked at me, then out the window again. After a minute he walked over behind the counter. "Let me know if ya need anything else," he said.

While my dad was gone I tried to imagine who this fellow Mason was. I figured he must be some guy hiding out from the Chicago cops, and that his real name probably wasn't Mason. My dad came back in less than an hour, picked up his change from the counterman, tipped him, and said to me, "Had enough to eat?" I said yes and followed him out to the car.

"This is an awfully small town," I said to my dad as we drove away. "Does Mason live here?" "Who?" he asked. Then he said, "Oh yeah, Mason." Dad didn't say anything else for a while. He took a cigar out of his overcoat pocket, bit off the tip, rolled down his window, and spit it out before saying, "No he doesn't live here. Just visiting."

We drove along for a few miles before Dad lit his cigar, leaving the window open. I put the scarf up around my face to keep warm and settled back in the seat. My dad drove and didn't talk for about a half hour. Around Marengo he said, "Did that counterman back there ask you any questions?" "He asked me if you were my dad and if we were from Chicago," I said. "What did you tell him?" "I said yes."

"Anything else?" "He asked if you were there for any special reason and I said you were there to see someone." "Did you tell him who?" Dad asked. "I said I didn't know his name."

Dad nodded and threw his dead cigar out the window, then rolled it up. "You tired?" he asked. "No," I said. "What do you think," he said, "would you rather live out here or in the city?" "The city," I said. "I think it's more interesting there." "So do I," said Dad. "Relax, son, and we'll be home before you know it."

A Rainy Day at the Nortown Theater

When I was about nine or ten years old my dad picked me up from school one day and took me to the movies. I didn't see him very often since my parents were divorced and I lived with my mother. This day my dad asked me what I wanted to do and since it was raining hard we decided to go see *Dragnet* starring Jack Webb and an Alan Ladd picture, *Shane*.

During the show my dad bought me a Holloway Slo-Poke caramel sucker and buttered popcorn. I had already seen *Dragnet* twice and since it wasn't such a great movie I was really interested in seeing *Shane*, which I'd already seen as well, but only once, and had liked it, especially the end where the kid, Brandon de Wilde, goes running through the bulrushes calling for Shane to come back, "Come back, Shane! Shane, come back!" I had really remembered that scene and was anxious to see it again, so all during *Dragnet* I kept still because I thought my dad wanted to see it, not having already seen it, and when *Shane* came on I was happy.

But it was Wednesday and my dad had promised my mother he'd have me home for dinner at six, so at about a quarter to, like I had dreaded in the back of my head, my dad said we had to go.

"But Dad," I said "*Shane's* not over till six-thirty and I want to see the end where the kid goes running after him yelling, 'Come back, Shane!' That's the best part!"

But my dad said no, we had to go, so I got up and went with him but walked slowly backward up the aisle to see as much of the picture as I could even though I knew now I wasn't going to get to see the end, and we were in the lobby, which was dark and red with gold curtains, and saw it was still pouring outside. My dad made me put on my coat and duck my head down into it when we made a run for the car, which was parked not very far away.

My dad drove me home and talked to me but I didn't hear what he said. I was thinking about the kid who would be running after Shane in about ten more minutes. I kissed my dad good-bye and went in to eat dinner but I stood in the hall and watched him drive off before I did.

The Back-to-School
Blacks and Blues

My dad never knew what I went through in school while
he was alive and I'm glad he didn't. I never talked
about it, he never asked, and it was just as well. I don't know
what he would have done. The worst day of school was
always the first. In Chicago we usually went back to school
the first day after Labor Day. The weather was still good and
it was something of a shock to the system—both physiologi-
cally and psychologically—to all of a sudden be cooped up in
a stuffy classroom after two and a half months of virtually
unmitigated freedom. Even if a kid worked a summer job it
wasn't the same as being confined in a tomblike enclosure
along with thirty or forty other suffering, sweating, restless
prisoners of the Board of Education while a teacher barked
away, oblivious to your discomfort.

I have three distinct memories of the occasion, that
excruciatingly difficult reentry to pedagogic reality. On the
first day of fifth grade, in the middle of the afternoon, Mr.
Mooth, the head maintenance man and janitor of DeWitt
Clinton Grammar School, a San Quentin–like institution

built a few minutes after the Fall of Rome, came into our room and without saying a word to the teacher told all of the boys to stand up next to their seat. Herman Mooth was a large man in his fifties who'd been the janitor and boiler-room mechanic at Clinton School for thirty years. He always wore the same clothes: a woolen checked shirt, baggy brown bum pants held up by suspenders, and steel-toed park ranger shoes. In one back pocket he had a crumpled, filthy gray handkerchief half sticking out and in the other he carried a dark brown half-pint bottle of rye whiskey. He had a grizzled gray mustache with hair to match—always worn a little bit too long, which in those days, the midfifties, was considered eccentric—and a perpetual scowl. All of the kids were afraid of him—the teachers probably were, too—and we stayed out of his way when he walked across the school yard from the maintenance shack to the main building. Rumor had it that Mooth once caught a little kid who'd thrown a snowball at his head and held him upside down in front of the open school coal-furnace door for an hour before letting him go. Mr. Mooth never wore a coat, not even when it was ten or twenty degrees below zero in the middle of February; and in the hot months he always wore the same long-sleeved woolen shirt with the cuffs unbuttoned. So when Mooth came into our room that hot, sticky September day in 1957 everyone, even Miss Lawson, our classic old maid–type teacher, was taken aback.

"You, you, and you!" Mooth shouted at three of us boys, including me. "You stand! The others sit!" he commanded. Pointing a stubby, swollen index finger at us he said, "I saw you three punks smoking in the school yard at eight o'clock last night. This is private property. If I catch you little jerks here again I'll get you sent to Bridewell"—the juvenile prison—"You got me?" The room was silent, nobody moved. Mooth stood there, pointing that grease-stained digit at us, his little red eyes boiling in the sunny classroom. I could see the dust motes floating past them. Then I spoke, "That wasn't me, Mr. Mooth," I said. "I wasn't in the school yard last night. And I don't smoke."

Mooth moved with the speed of a panther. He was at my desk before I knew what was happening and he slapped me hard across the face. "Don't!" he bellowed at me, sticking his flat fingertip into my chest. "Don't lie to me! I saw you! I can't prove it but you and your punk pals were smoking. I got all the butts as evidence!" Every eye in the classroom was on me. I didn't move one hair on my not-yet eleven-year-old head. Mooth stood in front of me for a full minute or more, breathing heavily, his whiskey breath blasting its way up my nostrils. I stopped breathing. Suddenly Mooth turned and walked out, slamming the door behind him. Old Miss Lawson, who was tall and skinny and wore a black dress every day, stared hard at me through her thick spectacles. I was branded in her eyes as a Bad Kid. Nothing I could say or do would dig me out of the hole Mr. Mooth had shoved me

into. I knew that year would be a long haul, and it was. I
never had a chance.

My second and third most vivid memories of back-to-
school adventures both occurred on the same day, my first
day of high school. I was sitting in the first row, listening to
Mr. Vincenzo, the algebra teacher, define the word equa-
tion, when a white 1950 Ford pickup truck pulled up on the
lawn outside the classroom window. A guy I recognized
immediately as Big Arv Nielsen jumped out of the driver's
side, leaving the motor running. There was a hole in the
truck's muffler so the rumble of the engine was deafening—
the belches and bops of the souped-up V-6 invaded the open
classroom windows as dramatically as, thirty seconds later,
Big Arv came tearing through the door the same way
Herman Mooth had done in Miss Lawson's room at Clinton
School four years before.

Big Arv, a heavyset, six-foot-tall Swedish kid—his full
name was Arvid, but nobody called him that—was three
years older than I. He'd gone to Clinton, too, and I remembered him there hanging out with another blond, crew-cut
kid named Oscar Fomento who got thrown out of grammar
school for setting a teacher's dress on fire. Big Arv wore
black Chippewa motorcycle boots and kept his flattop with
fenders even in the winter, never even wearing earmuffs, let
alone a hat. Arv was never mean to the younger kids,
though, the way his buddy Oscar Fomento had been, so I'd
always thought well of him. I mean, he could have been

mean if he'd wanted to. But he charged into the room and began choking Mr. Vincenzo, shoving him up against the blackboard. Vincenzo was taller than Arv Nielsen by three or four inches, and he was an athletic-looking thirty-year-old, but Big Arv was much more powerful and he held the algebra teacher up with one hand around the throat while he took a piece of paper out of his back pocket.

"You flunked me, Vincenzo!" Big Arv shouted, and he began slapping Vincenzo across the face with the piece of paper. "You flunked me in summer school," he yelled, "and now I can't come back here! I'll really get you for this, spaghetti head!" Then Arv released him and Vincenzo slumped to the floor. Big Arv sneered at the fallen man and spat on him. He crumpled the piece of paper, which must have been Nielsen's notice from the school that he'd flunked out, and tossed it down at Vincenzo. Big Arv looked around the classroom for a moment. All of the kids were frozen in their seats. He stared for a second directly at me in the front row, then he curled his lip, smoothed down the greased back sides of his head, and bolted out the door as fast as he entered. All of the kids ran to the windows and watched Big Arv clomp across the lawn in his boots, climb into the percolating pickup truck, jam it into low, and zoom off, tearing long divots in the grass. We looked back at Vincenzo. He got up off the floor slowly, shook himself like a wet dog, and then ran out of the room.

I never did see Big Arv Nielsen after that day, but twenty years later a friend of mine from the old neighborhood mentioned to me that he'd heard Arv was living in Japan on the proceeds of an investment he'd made in a Broadway musical. Big Arv was apparently a wealthy man, doing just fine despite his adolescent difficulties with algebra.

My third most memorable event was not as traumatic as the run-in with Mr. Mooth or as entertaining as Big Arv Nielsen's attack on Mr. Vincenzo, but just as unforgettable. After classes let out that first day of high school, I attempted to help my friend Eddie in a fight he was having with three guys in front of school. I grabbed the shoulder of one of the boys and pulled him off, but just as I did one of Eddie's feet kicked up and he hit me smack in the nose with the heel of his boot. Blood sprayed out all over the place. It felt like my nose had exploded—it was broken. To this day I carry a bump on the bridge of my nose from that fight.

Sometimes I try to be fair-minded about school, to place these and other events in proper perspective. Could these early school years really have been as ridiculous and absurd—and painful—as I remember them? Any school kid could answer that.

Letter from Larry

Monday Nite

Hello Boy—

Thank you for your nice letter. Youse guys must have been eating too much candy! Huh? That's the reason the candy was taken away. Yes? No? I'll betcha!!

Also—it's good to hear that you have rid yourself of that cold, and you now feel "very good."

We, here at home, miss you. But, we hope you are at least having some fun. Otherwise, the whole deal is "No Good." How about it?

Mother tells me that she wrote a note to you today, and in it she told you about our sailing trip with your uncle Buck. But—I don't think your mother gave you all the "horrible" details. So—I shall do so!—Are you listening, Boy?

First, let me tell you that Uncle Buck has a beaut of a sailboat. It's really keen! It's 27 feet long, has a real high mast, which carries a big spread of mainsail—and also a high jib sail. This boat was made in Sweden—and it can really travel fast.

Well, 2 Sundays ago—Mother, Pops, and I went sailing on the "Friendship" *(that's the name of the boat) with Uncle Buck. It was too calm (no breeze) for fast sailing, so we just "horsed around" the lake for the afternoon without any danger or excitement.*

But—*yesterday (Sunday) we went sailing again! There was your cousin Darlene and her boyfriend, Chris, and Uncle Buck and Mother and I.*

It looked sort of rough on the lake. The waves were high, and there was a strong northeast wind.—But—in spite of all that we went out—and man—it was rough!

We had full sails on. I was up forward hanging on a mast stay for dear life, and the waves kept coming over the deck, soaking me from head to feet. Of course, all I wore was bathing shorts.

The wind kept us keeled over, so that one side of the boat was high up and the other side was under the water. It sorta scared Mother, a bit—And I'll tell you a secret, it scared me too, tho I'll never admit it!

It kept getting rougher and rougher. We saw another sail-boat ram into a cabin cruiser, snapping the mast and they had to be rescued.

Anyway, Boy, there were a few times I thought I'd fall in the water. But—I hung on with a leg wrapped around a stay.

Finally, one of the mast stays broke—and we were lucky to have the wind on our side, because we had to take down all the sails, and the wind blew us towards the harbor, where we got a tow to our anchorage. It was a rough trip—But all's well that ends well.

Mom has a cold from the windy trip—But, we will see that she shakes it off.

The McLaughlin kids say "Hello." They want to know when you are getting back here.

All's well, son. Take care of yourself.

Our Love To You

Your,

Larr

I READ THE LETTER OVER AND OVER. It was written to me when I was about nine or ten while I was up in Wisconsin at summer camp by my mother's second husband, Larry. It's a horrible story. They were married six months; he was tall and handsome, an Irishman, Lucius Larry Cohan, George M. Cohan's nephew, he said.

I really loved him. Not the same as the way I loved my dad, but he and I played together all the time; he never had to discipline me, I always did what Larry wanted because he was such a great guy, and I knew my mother loved him because he was so handsome and smart. A great athlete, trim and hard, Larry was nearly fifty, maybe more, but looked ten or more years younger. We were really happy, my mother and Larry and I, during this six months.

Then one day Larry refused to get out of bed. Like Bartleby, he just preferred not to get up. My mother went running out to our cousins' house semihysterical, absolutely at a loss as to what to do. I was home sick from school that day. I sat in the room and watched him. Larry just lay there. When people came to talk to him he would nod, or just whisper a wistful "No."

He stared, not vacantly, but mournfully, an eerie but not frightening—to me, anyway—saddened stare, like he knew. Not in any hierarchical sense, but as if he felt there was nothing to do but lie there, looking up at the ceiling. Finally my mother took me away and told me to stay in another room.

I didn't know what was happening. Eventually my mother made Larry leave, forced him to slowly put on socks and pants and shirt and shoes and walk out. He did it as if he were in a dream, in dream-motion, not really there at all. He was vapor; standing, walking, even lying there was some irreality, not conscious action. He was looking around for the angels.

My mother later found out from Larry's sister in Charleston, West Virginia, that he had been wounded and shell-shocked in the war. He had married my mother after being released from the VA hospital, never told her, and had a metal plate in his head. He wasn't allowed to drive because of it.

He went to stay in The Cass, a run-down fleabag hotel on the Near North Side of Chicago. My mother and I picked him up there one day and we went to the park. Larry begged my mother to take him back, that he'd be all right; and she was tempted because he was so handsome and all, but now weak and vague and unshaven, obviously struggling terribly. Even I, at eight years old, could see this.

I was half-frightened of him then because of his strange, bedraggled appearance and lost-soul incoherence. We were going to lunch, walking to the restaurant, and Larry said, "Where are we going now?" My mother said, "We're going to the restaurant to eat lunch, like you suggested." "That's a good idea," Larry said, "let's go eat lunch."

Naturally this scared my mother, who was still young, only twenty-nine, and under the thumb of relatives in those days who were warning her, telling her not to take him back. (Many were just jealous because, when sane, Larry was so sharp, too fast for them and made them uncomfortable. Also, his handsomeness disturbed my mother's ugly women relatives, who were envious.) So, my mother divorced him, and I never saw him again.

The Trophy

My dad was not much of an athlete. I don't recall his ever playing catch with me or doing anything requiring particular athletic dexterity. I knew he was a kind of tough guy because my mother told me about his knocking other guys down now and again, but he wasn't interested in sports. He did, however, take me to professional baseball and football games and boxing matches but those were, for him, more like social occasions, opportunities to meet and be greeted by business associates and potential customers. At Marigold Arena or the Amphitheater Dad spent most of his time talking to people rather than watching the event. He may have gone bowling on occasion but never in my company.

When I was nine I joined a winter bowling league. I was among the youngest bowlers in the league and certainly the youngest on my team. The league met on Saturday mornings at Nortown Bowl on Devon Avenue between Maplewood and Campbell Streets. The lanes were on the second floor up a long, decrepit flight of stairs above Crawford's Department Store. I told my dad about it and invited him to come watch me bowl. I wasn't very good, of course, but I took it seriously, as I did all competitive sports, and I steadily improved. I practiced after school a couple of times during the week with older guys, who gave me tips on how to improve my bowling skills.

There were kids who practically lived at the bowling alley. Most of them were sixteen or older and had pretty much given up on formal education. The state law in Illinois held that public education was mandatory until the age of sixteen; after that, a kid could do whatever he wanted until he was eighteen, at which time he was required to register for military service. It was the high school dropouts who got drafted right away; but for two years these guys got to sleep late and spend their afternoons and evenings hanging out at the bowling alley, betting on games, and gorging themselves on Italian beef sandwiches. At night they would go to Uptown Bowl, where the big, often televised professional matches took place.

The announcer for these events was usually Whispering Ray Rayburn, a small, weaselish man who wore a terrible brown toupee and pencil-line mustache. His ability to speak into a microphone at a consistently low but adequately audible decibel level was his claim to fame. Kids, including myself, often imitated Whispering Ray as they toed the mark preparatory to and as they took their three- or four-step approach before releasing the bowling ball:

"Zabrofsky casually talcs his right hand," a kid would whisper to himself as he stood at the ball rack, "slips three digits into the custom-fit Brunswick Black Beauty, hefts the sixteen-pound spheroid"—(one of Whispering Ray's favorite words for the ball was "spheroid")—"balances it delicately in the palm of his left hand. Amazing how Zabrofsky handles the ebony orb"—("orb" was another pet name)—"almost daintily, as if it were an egg. Now Zabrofsky steps to his spot, feet tight together. He needs this spare to keep pace with the leader, Lars Grotwitz. Zabrofsky studies the five-ten split that confronts him with the kind of concentration Einstein must have mustered to unmuzzle an atom." ("Muster" was also big in Whispering Ray's lexicon.) "Zabrofsky's breathing is all we can hear now. Remember, fans, Big Earl is an asthmatic who depends heavily on the use of an inhaler in order to compete. You can see the impression it makes in the left rear pocket of his Dacron slacks. Despite this serious handicap his intensity is impressive. He begins his approach: one, two, three, the ball swings back and as Big Earl slides forward on the fourth step the powerful form smoothly sets his spheroid on its way. Zabrofsky's velvet touch has set the ebony orb hurtling toward the kingpin. At the last instant it veers left as if by remote control, brushes the five as it whizzes past and hips it toward the ten. Ticked almost too softly, the ten wobbles like an habitué dismounting a stool at Johnny Fazio's Tavern"—(Johnny Fazio was a sponsor of the local TV broadcasts)—"then tumbles into the gutter! Zabrofsky makes the tough spare."

On the last Saturday in February, the league awarded trophies to be presented personally to each team member by Carmen Salvino, a national champion bowler. My team had won its division despite my low pin total. Each team had on its roster at least one novice bowler, leaving it up to the more experienced members to "carry" him, which my team had managed to do. I was grateful to my older teammates for their guidance, patience, and encouragement, and thanks to them I was to be awarded a trophy. The only guy on the team who had not been particularly generous toward me was Oscar Fomento, who worked part-time as a pinsetter. Fomento, not to my displeasure, had left the team two weeks into the league season, after having beaten up his parents with a bowling pin when they gave him a hard time about ditching school. One of the other guys told me Oscar had been sent to a reformatory in Colorado where they shaved his head and made him milk cows in below-freezing temperatures. "That's tough," my teammate said, "but just think how strong Fomento's fingers'll be when he gets back."

My dad had not made it to any of the Saturday morning matches, so I called him on Friday night before the last day of the league and told him this would be his final chance to see me bowl, and that Carmen Salvino would be there giving out trophies. I didn't tell Dad that I'd be receiving a trophy because I wanted him to be surprised. "Salvino," my Dad said. "Yeah, I know the guy. Okay, son."

It snowed heavily late Friday night and into Saturday morning. I had to be at Nortown Bowl by nine and flurries were still coming down at five-to when I kicked my way on a shortcut through fresh white drifts in the alley between Rockwell and Maplewood. Dashing up the steep wet steps I worried about Carmen Salvino and my father being able to drive there. I lived a block away, so it was easy for me and most of the other kids to walk over. I hoped the snowplows were out early clearing the roads.

During the games I kept watching for my dad. Toward the end of the last line there was a lot of shouting: Carmen Salvino had arrived. Our team finished up and went over with the other kids to the counter area, behind which hundreds of pairs of used bowling shoes, sizes two to twenty, were kept in cubbyholes similar to mail slots at hotel desks. Carmen Salvino, a tall, hairy-armed man with thick eyebrows and a head of hair the color and consistency of a major oil slick, stood behind the counter in front of the smelly, worn, multicolored bowling shoes between the Durkee brothers, Dominic and Don, owners of Nortown Bowl.

Dominic and Don Durkee were both about five foot six and had hair only on the sides of their heads, sparse blue threads around the ears. They were grinning like madmen because the great Carmen Salvino was standing next to them in their establishment. The Durkees' skulls shone bright pink under the rude fluorescent lights. The reflection from the top of Carmen Salvino's head blinded anyone foolish enough to stare at it for more than a couple of seconds.

I was the last kid to be presented a trophy. When Carmen Salvino gave it to me he shook my small, naked hand with his huge, hairy one. I noticed, however, that he had extremely long, slender fingers, like a concert pianist's. "Congrajalayshuns, son," he said to me. Then Carmen Salvino turned to Dominic Durkee and asked, "So, we done now?"

When I walked back home through the alley from Maplewood to Rockwell, the snow was still perfectly white and piled high in front of the garages. At home I put my trophy on the top of my dresser. It was the first one I had ever received. The trophy wasn't very big but I really liked the golden figure of a man holding a golden bowling ball, his right arm cocked back. He didn't look at all like Carmen Salvino, or like me, either. He resembled my next-door neighbor Jimmy McLaughlin, an older kid who worked as a dishwasher at Kow Kow's Chinese restaurant on the corner of Devon and Rockwell. Jimmy worked all day Saturday, I knew. I decided I'd take the trophy over later and show it to him.

The Piano Lesson

I bounced the ball against the yellow wall in the front of my house, waiting for the piano teacher. I'd been taking lessons for six weeks and I liked the piano, my mother played well, standards and show tunes, and sang. Often I sang along with her or by myself as she played. "Young at Heart" and "Bewitched, Bothered and Bewildered" were two of my favorites. I loved the dark blue cover of the sheet music of "Bewitched," with the drawing of the woman in a flowing white gown in the lower left-hand corner. It made me think of New York, though I'd never been there. White on midnight dark.

I liked to stand next to the piano bench while my mother played and listen to "Satan Takes a Holiday," a fox-trot it said on the sheet music. I was eight years old and could easily imagine foxes trotting in evening gowns.

I was up to "The Scissors-Grinder" and "Swan on the Lake" in the second red Thompson book. That was pretty good for six weeks, but I had begun to stutter. I knew I had begun to stutter because I'd heard my mother say it to my father on the phone. They ought just to ignore it, she'd said, and it would stop.

"Ready for your lesson today?" asked the teacher as she came up the walk.

"I'll be in in a minute," I said, continuing to bounce the ball off the yellow bricks. The teacher smiled and went into the building.

I kept hitting the ball against the wall. I knew she would be talking to my mother, then arranging the lesson books on the rack above the piano. I hit the ball once high above the first-floor windows, caught it, and ran.

Listening to the News

My favorite radio stations when I was a kid were WOPA and WAAF in Chicago, and WLAC in Nashville. This was during the fifties, when I'd lie awake in the small hours of the morning and dig Big Bill Hill's Shopping Bag Show on the weak Oak Park, Illinois, frequency. (WOPA was broadcast from the Oak Park Arms Hotel—thus the call letters "OPA.") Big Bill called it the Shopping Bag Show because he kept a shopping bag full of liquor bottles by his feet while he broadcast blues records. A listener could hear the bottles clanking against one another as he pulled one up and played a disc by Eddie Clearwater ("A-Minor Cha-cha") or the latest Magic Sam release on Crash or Cobra. More than once I heard him play a tune by, say, Eddie Boyd, then announce, "Man, I like that one so much I gone play it *again*. Don't care whether *nobody* else care for it. My opinion the onliest one that count!" And, of course, he'd spin Eddie Boyd until he got tired of it. Occasionally, Big Bill would do a remote from the Phoenix Club in Harvey, Illinois, where there was live music, like J.B. Hutto and the Hawks. Hutto was a marvelous slide guitarist and Big Bill loved the slide. "Play 'Hip-Shakin' again!" Bill would shout at him; inevitably, J.B. would oblige.

WAAF was highlighted for years by Daddio's Jazz Patio, an afternoon show hosted by Daddio Daylie, an acquaintance of my father's. Daddio played all kinds of records: blues, R & B, pop, jazz, soul—everything from James Brown to Jerry Lee Lewis. WAAF was a "black" station—on Sundays they broadcast church services—but Daddio didn't care about that; when he heard something he liked, he played it. This was in contrast to Purvis Spann over at WVON, a straight soul station, which I also loved. It was on WVON that I first heard the Valentinos do "Lookin' for a Love" by Bobby Womack. But Daddio Daylie had a personality that didn't quit. He became famous in Chicagoland to the extent that politicians fiercely contested for his endorsement.

WLAC played a combination of hillbilly, rock and roll, and pop. Since it was a fifty-thousand-watt AM channel I could get it at night either in Chicago or in Tampa, Florida, the two cities I lived in most often in those days. Randy's Record Shop in Murfreesboro, Tennessee, was the sponsor I remember best on WLAC. Randy's offered great deals on collections of 45s. I listened to and dug Pee Wee King, Bill Monroe, the Everly Brothers (they did a show out of Shenandoah, Iowa, I believe, with their father, Ike, that made it to Chicago—in fact, they may have broadcast from Chicago for a time), Jerry Lee (even after he married his thirteen-year-old cousin, Myra), and, of course, Elvis.

Living in the Midwest and the Deep South gave me access to stations from Macon, Georgia; Memphis, Tennessee;

Little Rock, Arkansas; even, on a clear night, New Orleans, Louisiana. The music that was broadcast during the fifties and early sixties changed and formed my existence. I'll never forget hearing the rhythm section intro to Little Richard's "Lucille"—that sound made me realize right then, at ten years old or however old I was, that the world truly had to be a wild and mysterious place. I wanted to find out where that sound came from, what made it happen. It cut into the deepest part of my being, as did, a few years later, Wilson Pickett's scream or Maria Callas's stunning and dangerous arias. Great art is always dangerous, daring the listener, viewer, or reader to go over the edge with the artist. The music I picked up on back in the days was like that, and I'm still listening for it. It's the real news.

The Aerodynamics
of an Irishman

There was a man who lived on my block when I was a kid whose name was Rooney Sullavan. He would often come walking down the street while the kids were playing ball in front of my house or Johnny McLaughlin's house. Rooney would always stop and ask if he'd ever shown us how he used to throw the knuckleball back when he pitched for Kankakee in 1930.

"Plenty of times, Rooney," Billy Cunningham would say. "No knuckles about it, right?" Tommy Ryan would say. "No knuckles about it, right!" Rooney Sullavan would say. "Give it here and I'll show you." One of us would reluctantly toss Rooney the ball and we'd step up so he could demonstrate for the fortieth time how he held the ball by his fingertips only, no knuckles about it.

"Don't know how it ever got the name knuckler," Rooney'd say. "I call mine the Rooneyball." Then he'd tell one of us, usually Billy because he had the catcher's glove—the old fat-heeled kind that didn't bend unless somebody stepped on it, a big black mitt that Billy's dad had handed down to him from his days at Kankakee or Rock Island or someplace—to get sixty feet away so Rooney could see if he could still "make it wrinkle."

Billy would pace off twelve squares of sidewalk, each square being approximately five feet long, the length of one nine-year-old boy's body stretched head to toe lying flat, squat down, and stick his big black glove out in front of his face. With his right hand he'd cover his crotch in case the pitch got away and short-hopped off the cement where he couldn't block it with the mitt. The knuckleball was unpredictable, not even Rooney could tell what would happen once he let it go.

"It's the air makes it hop," Rooney claimed. His leather jacket creaked as he bent, wound up, rotated his right arm like nobody'd done since Chief Bender, crossed his runny gray eyes, and released the ball from the tips of his fingers. We watched as it sailed straight up at first, then sort of floated on an invisible wave before plunging the last ten feet like a balloon that had been pierced by a dart.

Billy always went down on his knees, the back of his right hand stiffened over his crotch, and stuck out his gloved hand at the slowly whirling Rooneyball. Just before it got to Billy's mitt the ball would give out entirely and sink rapidly, inducing Billy to lean forward in order to catch it, only he couldn't because at the last instant it would take a final, sneaky hop before bouncing surprisingly hard off of Billy's unprotected chest.

"*Just* like I told you," Rooney Sullavan would exclaim. "All it takes is plain old air."

Billy would come up with the ball in his upturned glove, his right hand rubbing the place on his chest where the pitch had hit. "You all right, son?" Rooney would ask, and Billy would nod. "Tough kid," Rooney'd say. "I'd like to stay out with you fellas all day, but I got responsibilities." Rooney would muss up Billy's hair with the hand that held the secret to the Rooneyball and walk away whistling "When Irish Eyes Are Smiling" or "My Wild Irish Rose." Rooney was about forty-five or fifty years old and lived with his mother in a bungalow at the corner. He worked nights for Wanzer Dairy, washing out returned milk bottles.

Tommy Ryan would grab the ball out of Billy's mitt and hold it by the tips of his fingers like Rooney Sullavan did, and Billy would go sit on the stoop in front of the closest house and rub his chest. "No way," Tommy would say, considering the prospect of his ever duplicating Rooney's feat. "There must be something he's not telling us."

Dark Mink

Pops, my other grandfather, my mother's father, and his brothers spent much of their time playing bridge and talking baseball in the back room of their fur coat business. From the time I was four or five Pops would set me up on a high stool at a counter under a window looking down on State Street and give me a furrier's knife with a few small pelts to cut up. I spent whole afternoons that way, wearing a much-too-large-for-me apron with the tie strings wrapped several times around my waist, cutting up mink, beaver, fox, squirrel, even occasional leopard or seal squares, careful not to slice my finger with the razor-sharp mole-shaped tool, while the wet snow slid down the high, filthy State and Lake Building windows and Pops and my great-uncles Ike, Nate, and Louie played cards.

They were all great baseball fans, they were gentlemen, and didn't care much for other sports, so even in winter the card table tended to be hot-stove league speculation about off-season trades or whether or not Sauer's legs would hold up for another season. Of course there were times customers came in, well-to-do women with their financier husbands, looking as if they'd stepped out of a Peter Arno *New Yorker* cartoon; or gangsters with their girlfriends, heavy-overcoated guys with thick cigars wedged between leather-gloved fingers. I watched the women model the coats and straighten their stocking seams in the four-sided full-length mirrors. I liked dark mink the best, those ankle-length, full-collar, silk-lined ones that smelled so good with leftover traces of perfume. There was no more luxurious feeling than to nap under my mother's own sixty-pelt coat.

By the time the fur business bottomed out, Pops was several years dead—he'd lived to eighty-two—and so was Uncle Ike, at eighty-eight. Pops had seen all of the old-time great ballplayers, Tris Speaker, the Babe, even Joe Jackson, who he said was the greatest player of them all. When the White Sox clinched the American League pennant in 1959, the first flag for them in forty years (since the Black Sox scandal of 1919), he and I watched the game on television. The Sox were playing Cleveland, and to end it the Sox turned over one of their 141 double plays of that season, Aparicio to Fox to Big Ted Kluszewski.

Uncle Nate and Uncle Louie kept on for some time, going in to work each day not as furriers but to Uncle Louie's Chicago Furriers Association office. He'd founded the association in the '20s, acting as representative to the Chamber of Commerce, Better Business Bureau, and other civic organizations. Louie was also a poet. He'd written verse, he told me, in every form imaginable. Most of them he showed me were occasional poems, written to celebrate coronations—

the brothers had all been born and raised in London—and inaugurations of American presidents. In the middle right-hand drawer of his desk he kept boxes of Dutch-shoe chocolates, which he would give me whenever I came to visit him.

Uncle Nate, who lived to be 102, came in to Uncle Louie's office clean-shaven and with an impeccable high-starched collar every day until he was a hundred. He once told me he knew he would live that long because of a prophecy by an old man in a wheelchair he'd helped cross a London street when he was seven. The man had put his hand on Nate's head, blessed him, and told him he'd live a century.

Uncle Louie was the last to go, at ninety-four. Having long since moved away, I didn't find out about his death until a year or so later. The fur business, as my grandfather and his brothers had known it, was long gone; even the State and Lake Building was about to be torn down, a fate that had already befallen Fritzl's, where the brothers had gone each day for lunch. Fritzl's had been the premier restaurant of the Loop in those days, with large leather booths, big white linen napkins, and thick, high-stemmed glasses. Like the old Lindy's in New York, Fritzl's was frequented by show people, entertainers, including ballplayers, and newspaper columnists. Many of the women who had bought coats, or had had coats bought for them, at my grandfather's place ate there. I was always pleased to recognize one of them, drinking a martini or picking at a shrimp salad, the fabulous dark mink draped gracefully nearby.

The Pitcher

One night when I was eleven I was playing baseball in the alley behind my house. I was batting left-handed when I hit a tremendous home run that rolled all the way to the end of the alley and would have gone into the street but an old man turning the corner picked it up. The old man came walking up the alley toward me and my friends, flipping the baseball up in the air and catching it. When he got to where we stood, the old man asked us who'd hit that ball.

"I did," I said.

"It was sure a wallop," said the old man, and he stood there, grinning. "I used to play ball," he said, and my friends and I looked at each other. "With the Cardinals, and the Cubs."

My friends and I looked at the ground or down the alley where the cars went by on Rosemont Avenue.

"You don't believe me," said the old man. "Well, look here." And he held out a gold ring in the palm of his hand. "Go on, look at it," he said. I took it. "Read it," said the old man.

"World Series, 1931," I said.

"I was with the Cardinals then," the old guy said, smiling now. "Was a pitcher. These days I'm just an old bird dog, a scout."

I looked up at the old man. "What's your name?" I asked.

"Tony Kaufmann," he said. I gave him his ring back. "You just keep hitting 'em like that, young fella, and you'll be a big leaguer." The old man tossed my friend Billy the ball. "So long," he said, and walked on up to the end of the alley, where he went in the back door of Beebs and Glen's Tavern.

"Think he was tellin' the truth or is he a nut?" one of the kids asked me.

"I don't know," I said, "let's go ask my grandfather. He'd remember him if he really played."

Billy and I ran into my house and found Pops watching TV in his room.

"Do you remember a guy named Tony Kaufmann?" I asked him. "An old guy in the alley just told us he pitched in the World Series."

"He showed us his ring," said Billy.

My grandfather raised his eyebrows. "Tony Kaufmann? In the alley? I remember him. Sure, he used to pitch for the Cubs."

Billy and I looked at each other.

"Where's he now?" asked my grandfather.

"We saw him go into Beebs and Glen's," said Billy.

"Well," said Pops, getting out of his chair, "let's go see what the old-timer has to say."

"You mean you'll take us in the tavern with you?" I asked.

"Come on," said Pops, not even bothering to put on his hat, "never knew a pitcher who could hold his liquor."

Death at the Ballpark

A fat guy fell out of the stands into the Kansas City Royals bullpen during the ninth inning of the seventh game of the American League Championship Playoffs at Exhibition Stadium in Toronto in 1985. I watched on TV as he lay there with his gut sticking out from under his shirt in a puddle of water while the Kansas City pitchers stood around looking at him and up into the seats and wondered how he got there. The guy looked dead. He wasn't moving and from twenty-five hundred miles away through the miracle of electronic satellite transmission it looked to me like he wasn't breathing either. The Bluejays were behind in the game by four runs in the bottom of the ninth and it was obvious they'd blown their opportunity to meet the St. Louis Cardinals in the World Series when the fat guy landed on the field. It was several minutes before a medical crew reached the body but eventually four men managed to lift him onto a stretcher and carry him off through a door in the outfield fence.

The crowd was getting rowdy at this point because they knew the season was finished for their team. Not too many of them paid attention to the fat dead-looking guy. The TV cameras shifted suddenly from the bullpen to the Toronto Bluejays dugout. The players weren't paying much attention to the guy either; they sat staring at their shoes or their fingernails or just off into space, probably thinking about what they would say to their wives and kids and girlfriends when they got home. Undoubtedly some of them were wondering where they would be playing next year.

The incident reminded me of the time my dad and I were at a Chicago Bears football game at Wrigley Field on an ice-cold December day in 1956, when I was ten, and a fat guy carrying two large beers collapsed on the stairs in the aisle next to us. The beer splashed down the steps and froze, turning the snow green. The guy didn't even groan, he just lay on his back covering three steps like the man in the Kansas City bullpen did twenty-nine years later. My dad said to me that the guy must have had a heart attack or something and died on the spot because he wasn't moving.

Two Andy Frain ushers came running down the steps and looked at the guy. They tried to lift him up but he was too heavy; he kept slipping out of their hands but they kept trying to move him. He must have weighed close to three hundred pounds. Some fans seated behind us started shouting at the ushers to get out of the way, that they were blocking their view of the game. "Down in front!" the fans yelled. The ushers looked around helplessly. They were two tall skinny guys with bad complexions shivering in their short blue usher's jackets. Their ears were red from the cold, their noses ran. Nobody moved to help them. "Leave the guy!" someone shouted. "It's ten goddamn degrees below zero. He won't start stinking until June!"

Finally my dad and another guy got up and helped the ushers drag the dead man up the stairs to a landing where a third usher covered him with a blanket. This happened about midway through the third period. I kept looking back at the landing to see if they'd taken the body away but he was still there at the start of the fourth quarter. The game got exciting and I didn't check back again until just before the game ended and saw the body was gone.

As we filed up the stairs on our way out of the stadium I looked over at the spot on the landing where they'd covered him up: there was nothing there but a patch of flat, dirty snow. The people around us were talking about the game, about the great catch Harlon Hill had made to put the Bears ahead, or the twisting, acrobatic forty-yard run the Detroit halfback Hopalong Cassady had made with a desperation screen pass. Most of the crowd didn't even know about the fat guy who had died on the steps by our seats. All they wanted to do was get into their cars and warm up.

The Wedding

When my mother married her third husband, I, at the age of eleven, was given the duty, or privilege, of proposing a toast at the banquet following the wedding. My uncle Buck coached me—"Unaccustomed as I am to public speaking," I was to begin.

I kept going over it in my head. "Unaccustomed as I am to public speaking . . ." until the moment arrived and I found myself standing with a glass in my hand saying, "Unaccustomed as I am to public speaking—" I stopped. I couldn't remember what else my uncle had told me to say, so I said, "I want to propose a toast to my new father"—I paused—"and my old mother."

Everybody laughed and applauded. I could hear my uncle's high-pitched twitter. It wasn't what I was supposed to have said, that last part. My mother wasn't old, she was about thirty, and that wasn't what I'd meant by "old." I'd meant she was my same mother, that hadn't changed. No matter how often the father changed the mother did not.

I was afraid I'd insulted her. Everybody laughing was no insurance against that. I didn't want this new father, and a few months later, neither did my mother.

A Place in the Sun

The final memory I have of my dad is the time we attended a Chicago Bears football game at Wrigley Field about a month before he died. It was in November of 1958, a cold day, cold even for November on the shore of Lake Michigan. I don't remember what team the Bears were playing that afternoon; mostly I recall the overcast sky, the freezing temperature and visible breath of the players curling out from beneath their helmets like smoke from dragons' nostrils.

My dad was in good spirits despite the fact that the colostomy he'd undergone that previous summer had measurably curtailed his physical activities. He ate heartily at the game, the way he always had: two or three hot dogs, coffee, beer, a few shots of Bushmill's from a flask he kept in an overcoat pocket. He shook hands with a number of men on our way to our seats and again on our way out of the stadium, talking briefly with each of them, laughing and patting them on the back or arm.

Later, however, on our way home, he had to stop the car and get out to vomit on the side of the road. After he'd finished it took him several minutes to compose himself, leaning back against the door until he felt well enough to climb back in behind the wheel. "Don't worry, son," he said to me. "Just a bad stomach, that's all."

During the summer, after my dad got out of the hospital, we'd gone to Florida, where we stayed for a few weeks in a house on Key Biscayne. I had a good time there, swimming in the pool in the yard and watching the boats navigate the narrow canal that ran behind the fence at the rear of the property. I liked waving to and being waved at by the skippers as they guided their sleek white powerboats carefully through the inlet. One afternoon, though, I went into my dad's bedroom to ask him something and I saw him in the bathroom holding the rubber pouch by the hole in his side through which he was forced to evacuate his bowels. He grimaced as he performed the necessary machinations and told me to wait for him outside. He closed the bathroom door and I went back to the pool.

I sat in a beach chair looking out across the inland waterway in the direction of the Atlantic Ocean. I didn't like seeing my dad look so uncomfortable, but I knew there was nothing I could do for him. I tried to remember his stomach the way it was before, before there was a red hole in the side of it, but I couldn't. I could only picture him as he stood in the bathroom moments before with the pain showing in his face.

When he came out he was dressed and smiling. "What do you think, son?" he said. "Should I buy this house? Do you like it here?"

I wanted to ask him how he was feeling now, but I didn't. "Sure, Dad," I said. "It's a great place."

The Fighters

Whenever I was sick at home in bed when I was a boy my dad would bring me comic books. Sometimes I was too sick to look at them but it made me feel better knowing that there were piles of comics next to me and on the floor by the side of the bed.

After the divorce my dad saw me only once or twice a week. We lived near each other, which made visiting easy, but he worked long hours and didn't really have very much time to spare away from his business. I understood this and since he and my mother were on friendly terms and spoke well of one another in the other's absence I had no difficulty in accepting the situation.

The time I was very sick with pneumonia Dad brought me a great many comic books—*Submariner*, *Superboy*, *Fantastic Four*—and sat by me on the bed and wiped my forehead with a cold washcloth. He kidded with me as he usually did, telling me I'd be up playing football in a couple of days, but he kept his voice down, that was different. He stood talking with my grandfather, my mother's father who lived with me and my mother, in the doorway of my room for what seemed like a long time.

Dad came over to me again before he left and picked up my hand. He looked at me until I opened my eyes. "Come on, boy," he said. "You remember Gumbo Roux, don't you? The welter from Morgan City?" I nodded yes. Dad had taken me to see him fight for the title at Graceland Arena when I was nine. "He had rickets when he was a kid," Dad said. "Pneumonia, too, everything. His family was so poor. And didn't he turn out okay! The way he snapped that hook on McKee."

I wanted to ask my dad what rickets were, but I was too weak to talk. He was grinning at me, remembering McKee coming up off his feet for a second, then flying left on his ear against the top rope before falling for good. "You'll be okay," dad said. He squeezed my hand and my eyes closed again. I had an autographed picture of Gumbo Roux Dad had gotten for me—"To a Future Champ from The Champ" Gumbo Roux had written across his legs—but I couldn't remember where I'd put it.

I never saw my dad when he was sick, he wouldn't let me, and I didn't see him for several days before he died. My mother was going out one evening when she reminded me to call him in the hospital. She went out and I didn't call. The next afternoon, when I came home from school, my mother told me that my dad had died that morning. My grandfather, who had liked my dad very much, sat at the kitchen table, toast crumbs in his lap, staring into his teacup.

"You never called him last night like I told you to," said my mother. "Did you?"

I walked through the house into the living room and looked out the front window. Nothing was moving. I imagined my dad's big blue car coming down the street, Dad driving, a big cigar in his teeth, one hand on the wheel, the other right-angled out the open window, fingers gripping the roof. My mother came into the room and started talking. At that precise moment time began to pass more quickly.

The Delivery

I went up the stairs carrying the two shopping bags full of Chinese food figuring on a fifty-cent tip. It was a good Sunday due to the rain, people stayed in. I had two more deliveries in the bicycle basket. I rang the third-floor doorbell and waited, feeling the sub gum sauce leak on the bottom of one of the bags.

A woman opened the door and told me to please put the bags on the kitchen table, pointing the way. I put down the bags and looked at the woman. She was wearing a half-open pink nightgown, her nipples standing out against the thin material. Her hair was black halfway down her head, the bottom half was bleached and stringy.

"How much is it?" she asked.

"Five dollars," I said, looking at her purpled cheeks and chin.

"Just wait here and I'll get it for you," she told me. "Be right back."

I looked around the kitchen. I was twelve years old and was not used to being alone in strange kitchens. There were dishes in the sink, and one of the elements of the overhead fluorescent light was burned out, giving the kitchen a dull, rosy glow, like the woman's face, and her nightgown.

The woman came back and gave me a fifty-dollar bill. She had put on a green nightgown similar to the one she'd had on before, and flicked her pink tongue back and forth through her purple lips.

"I don't have any change for this," I said. "Don't you have anything smaller?"

She smiled. "Well, I'll just go see!" she said, and went off again.

I sat down on the kitchen table. I was beginning to enjoy myself, and was disappointed when she returned in the same green nightgown. She handed me a twenty.

"Will this do?" she asked.

I dug in my pocket for the change but she stopped me.

"Don't bother, darling," she said, smiling, and put her hand on my wrist. Her nails were painted dark red, but looked lighter in the hazy glow. "Keep it all," she said, and took me by the hand to the front door.

She put my hand on her breast. I could feel a lump through the nightgown.

"Thank you very, very much," she said, heavily, like Lauren Bacall or Tallulah Bankhead. I thought she looked like Tallulah Bankhead except for her hair, which was more like Lauren Bacall's.

"You're welcome," I said, and she opened the door for me, letting me out.

It was still raining, but I stood for a minute under the Dutch elm tree where I'd left my bike and the bags of food covered by a small piece of canvas. I removed the cover from the bicycle and folded it over the bags in the basket. I felt the twenty-dollar bill in my pocket, and I smiled. If I could have two deliveries like this a day, I thought, just two.

The Funeral

When I went to my father's funeral I refused to ride in the family car. At the grave I almost smiled as the two cemetery workers lowered the coffin. Everyone is watching themselves, I thought. There was nothing to cry about. It was nonsense, this death. It was over, it went on. My tears were for someone else, I was never quite sure for whom.

My sister was married two weeks later. At the wedding dinner my old grandfather Ezra who wore a mustache and still had the candy stand under the elevated near the ballpark stood up to make a speech. He meant to congratulate my sister but began to say something about his son who had died. He couldn't finish and sat down. Everyone watched him.

When my mother told me my grandfather was sick I went to see him. Dying, the old man who used to give me and my friends free candy and gum from his stand asked me what I was going to be.

"A writer," I told him.

The old man kept coughing. "What is a writer?" he puked from the bed.

There is more he is disappointed in than me, I thought.

All of the relatives were furious with me. Why couldn't I have said I would be a doctor or an engineer, something my grandfather could understand, not a scribbler who lets his family starve?

An Unsentimental
Education

An Unsentimental Education

One typically blazing hot and muggy afternoon in the summer of 1959, when I was twelve and a half years old, my pal Vinnie and I wandered up to the A-rab's drugstore on 30th Street in Tampa, Florida, to get a Dr. Pepper and browse through the skin magazines and cheap paperbacks that the A-rab stocked in rotating wire racks next to the soda fountain. I'd nicknamed the drugstore owner the A-rab because he had a scimitar-shaped proboscis and often wore a white towel over his head to absorb the sweat. At first I liked to imagine that the A-rab had fled Riyadh or Abu Dhabi in order to escape decapitation for having violated some powerful sheik's favorite daughter. He certainly looked the type; but after having gotten to know him as well as I did it seemed more likely for him to have violated the sheik's favorite camel. In reality the A-rab was a Jew from New Jersey who, like most snowbirds, couldn't take the bad weather anymore. He was a weird bird, though, with a really bizarre, sick sense of humor. I once named a pet alligator after him.

Vinnie and I often walked up to the A-rab's place to relieve the boredom of those long, unbearably humid days. We liked to sip our Dr. Peppers and read passages to each other from such immortal sleazeball paperback classics as *Sin Doll* by Orrie Hitt, and *Four Boys, a Girl and a Gun* by Willard Weiner. On this particular afternoon, however, after first having been greeted by the A-rab in his usual genteel fashion ("Hey, kid, know why God invented women?" "No, why?" "Sheep couldn't do the dishes."), Vinnie or I plucked from the rack a faded-blue Gold Medal novel by a man named Jim Thompson entitled *The Killer Inside Me.* "It was too bad about Joyce Lakeland," began a quote from the first inside page of the book. "If only she hadn't loved it when I beat her, the whole trouble wouldn't have started." Obviously, Vinnie and I agreed, we had stumbled onto something a little bit over the border from *Sin Doll.* This Jim Thompson sounded like the A-rab's kind of guy.

We killed the afternoon hanging out at the A-rab's reading the Thompson novel. It turned out to be a strange, unforgettable book about a small-town southern sheriff named Lou Ford who specialized in *boring* people to death before actually murdering a number of them. Ford's peculiar weapon was the platitude, clichés repeated over and over ("every cloud has a silver lining") while his victims, too frightened of Ford to run or rebuke, writhed in mute agony.

Walking home Vinnie said something that startled me: "Your dad was a killer, wasn't he?" "What do you mean?"

I asked angrily. "Why would you think that?" "Oh, just something I overheard your uncle say to your mother one day." "What was it?" "He was talking about Chicago," said Vinnie, "and why he left. 'You've got to be able to take care of somebody that needs taking care of,' he said. 'Rudy knew how to handle that kind of stuff, not me.' Something like that."

We walked the rest of the way without talking and after Vinnie turned off to go to his house I cut through the old boatyard to the river. I sat on the pier where earlier that summer my uncle had skinned the hide off an alligator some cracker had shot for table meat, and dangled my legs above the water. I thought about how my dad was dead now, and I couldn't ask him if he'd killed anybody. Nobody else could know for sure about something like that, I figured. Nobody could ever know for sure.

My Mother's People

My father was Jewish, and soon after his funeral my mother was approached by my father's family, who told her that the least she could do was to have me bar mitzvahed. "For Rudolph's sake," Esther, my father's sister, said. "He would have wanted his son to be bar mitzvahed."

She knew as well as I and my mother that Rudolph had not been at all religious. In fact, he had almost been ostracized by his family for marrying my mother, a Catholic. The marriage had not worked out because of family interference, mainly by my mother's mother, who didn't want her twenty-two-year-old daughter (my father was fifteen years older) running around with gangsters.

That part of it was true. My father ran an all-night liquor store on the corner of Chicago and Rush, next door to the Club Alabam, where I used to watch the showgirls rehearse on Saturday afternoons. I often ate breakfast at the small lunch counter in the store, dunking doughnuts with the organ-grinder's monkey. Big redheaded Louise ran the counter and fed me milk shakes while I waited for my dad. The place was a drop joint for stolen goods, dope, whatever somebody wanted to stash for a while. The story was that you could get anything at the store day or night. I used to see my dad giving guys penicillin shots in the basement, and I remember my mother throwing a fit when I was four years old sitting at three in the morning on a bundle of newspapers playing with a gun Bill Moore, a private cop, had given me to look at.

This kind of thing spooked my mother. My dad wore black shirts and gold ties, spoke with "dese" and "dose" and was famous for knocking guys through plate-glass windows. He'd done it twice—once in the newspaper the next day he'd been described as "that well-known man-about-town." Al Capone's brother, who was then using the name White, would come into the store often, as well as movie star Dorothy Lamour, ex–middleweight champ Tony Zale (who had a restaurant across the street—he used to show me the gloves from his matches), and whoever else was in town. We lived on Chestnut Street, next to the lake, in the Seneca Hotel, which was later described to me as containing "the lobby of the men with no last names."

My grandmother's fears were not unfounded. At one point, while my mother and father were vacationing in Hawaii, my dad received a phone call telling him some-body had been shot and that it would be best for them to extend their holiday. That was the first six-month absence of which I was aware. Later my parents spent a few months as the guest of Johnny Reata in Jamaica during another cooling-off period. Reata, my mother told me, had made his money running guns to Trujillo in the Dominican Republic.

While my mother, being a former University of Texas beauty queen, enjoyed the high-life aspects of being married to my father, the hoodlum end of it, plus the great influence her mother had over her, forced her to leave him, and I moved with her to the far North Side of the city. I continued to see my dad regularly until he died, and at no time did he ever so much as point out to me what a synagogue looked like, let alone tell me that he wanted me to be bar mitzvahed.

For some reason my mother allowed herself to be influenced by my aunt Esther and my dad's brother Bruno, both of whom were hypocritical Jews. Neither they, nor my uncle Joel, Esther's husband, who also interceded on my deceased father's behalf, and who once told me, looking me straight in the eye, that deep down inside 95 percent of the Gentiles hate the Jews and could not be trusted—including me, he meant, because of my mother—went to the synagogue except for High Holiday services; social appearances. They were stingy, mean, conniving people who had always been envious of my mother's good looks and power over my father, resenting the fact that my father had ever married her.

What made it so important that I be bar mitzvahed, they told my mother, was that I was the first son in the family. Both Bruno and Esther had had two girls apiece. I was the first one eligible to carry on the family name and tradition. And my father's father, the old man, my grandfather Ezra, who used to run numbers from his candy stand under the Addison Street el, was still alive. For his sake, before he passed away, they whined to my mother, I should be bar mitzvahed.

So my mother was persuaded. Her mother had died a few years before so there was no one to whom she could go for advice. I had to take Hebrew lessons. Three days a week after school I would sit with a little man who smelled of smoked fish, who spoke almost no English, and memorize words I did not understand. I also went to the synagogue each Saturday morning for nearly a year after my father died to say a prayer for him. My father's family insisted that I go, even though I had never been inside a synagogue before in my life. This was necessary, it was a son's duty, they explained, and my mother reluctantly acceded to their wishes. So on Saturdays I stood at the back of the temple, put on a black skullcap and recited a prayer written in English next to the Hebrew on a little pink card.

As the bar mitzvah day came closer I thought more and more about it, about why I was having to do this. Several times I told my mother I wouldn't go to Hebrew lessons anymore. None of it made sense to me, it was stupid, the whole thing was ridiculous. She knew I was right, but she told me to go through with it. "For your father's sake," she said. "My father's dead," I told her. "It doesn't matter to him and it wouldn't matter to him if he were alive."

But she said to finish it, then the debt to the family would be paid. This reasoning escaped me—I didn't see what we owed to them in the first place. But I stuck it out, and vowed that it really would be the end of it, that no one would ever make me do anything again.

After the bar mitzvah, which ritual I performed like an automaton, mouthing the lines as if I weren't really there, weren't the one doing it all, I did not see a member of my father's family—except briefly when my grandfather died—for seven years.

Passing through town those seven years later I went to see my dad's brother. Like my father, Uncle Bruno was a strong-willed, stubborn man. He had done well financially and kept his large brown brick house locked up like a fortress. When he saw me through the front-door window he motioned for me to come around the back way. "Too many bolts to undo in the front," he explained, as he and his wife admitted me through the rear entrance. They expressed their surprise at my being there, they hadn't recognized me right away. I told them I'd just come by to say hello, that was all.

Uncle Bruno insisted that I eat with them, they were just sitting down to dinner, which I did, and tell them what I'd been doing for the past few years. I gave them a brief history after which Uncle Bruno asked me if I'd come to see him about a job, or did I need money?

"I don't need any money," I told him, "and I have a job. I'm a writer," I said. My uncle looked annoyed and got up and walked into the living room and sat down. I followed him in and stood by the window. "Why did you come here

then, if you don't need any money?" he asked. "Out of curios-
ity," I said. Bruno lit a cigar. "Curious about what?" he said.

"Do you think things would have been different with me
had my father lived?" I asked. "Of course they would," Bruno
said. "You would have been a doctor or a lawyer or a pharmacist. Something important."

I knew it bothered Uncle Bruno that I didn't want any
money, or anything else, from him. It would have bothered
him had I asked for something but at least then he would
have had the satisfaction of being right.

"Then I'm glad he died when he did," I said, "before we
had any trouble about it."

"Being a Jew means nothing to you, does it?" said Uncle
Bruno. "You're one of your mother's people."

I realized I had no reason to be there, that I should never
have come. I put on my jacket.

"What did you expect?" I said, and left.

Uncle Buck

I've always loved my uncle Buck, my mother's brother, and after speaking to him on the telephone recently it occurred to me just how important a person he's always been to me; how I've always looked to him for an example of how I should live my life, especially in my father's absence.

As a teenager Buck rode an Indian motorcycle and did daredevil stunts at carnivals and fairs. In college—Georgia Tech—he captained the fencing team and was the Georgia state amateur golfing champion. After graduating with two engineering degrees, Buck went off to help build the railroad through the Yukon. He constructed bridges in Ireland, Portugal, and Burma, lumberjacked on Iron Mountain in Michigan, and during the war was in the Seabees as well as an operative in the OSS, winding up with the rank of full commander in the navy.

Since my mother's been married four times and my father died young. I suppose it was only natural that I'd fix on Uncle Buck as my most stable paternal figure. Physically, Buck has always been an impressive man: at seventy years old he still looks like a cross between Errol Flynn and Douglas Fairbanks Senior. He lived with us on and off while

I was a kid so I was able to spend a considerable amount of time with him. As a disciplinarian he was consistent and never unreasonable: if you did something wrong and didn't own up to it or whined about how rough or unfair things were, he took off his belt and used it. In that respect he was like the Ghurkas, the Nepalese soldiers who, once having removed their knives from their scabbards, even to clean them, could not replace them without drawing blood. Once Uncle Buck was pushed to the point of having taken off his belt, you knew nothing you might say or do short of running out and never coming back was going to prevent him from giving you a swipe or two across the rear. I'm convinced now that the actual physical punishment was not nearly so damaging as the psychological anguish caused by the sight of Uncle Buck beginning to unbuckle his belt.

Buck has always been quite a ladies' man. He can talk with ease to any woman and charm her. I actually used to more than half enjoy watching him "steal" my girlfriends away from me when I was fifteen and sixteen by his smile and engaging manner. I was always a willing student in Uncle Buck's school of How to Win and Influence Young Ladies though I could never hope to outdo the master.

Uncle Buck's first marriage, however, lasted only six years and ended badly; his wife found him with another woman and she divorced him. That marriage produced one son, my cousin Carl. Buck's second and last, to this point, official union lasted four years and ended even more rudely:

he caught his wife with another man and divorced her. That marriage produced one daughter, my cousin Christine. Buck's relationships with his children, both of whom were raised primarily by their mothers, have not been very successful. He demands a great deal of them, expecting them to be as independently minded and variously accomplished as he is and it has caused difficulties. Since I'm one step removed, a nephew, not a son or daughter, his attitude toward me has been more relaxed. We're friends as well as uncle and nephew, and there has been less pressure exerted by him on me to live up to any particular standards. When I finished high school he offered to help get me into the United States Naval Academy at Annapolis, and when I declined he didn't push the matter, even though I knew he would have liked me to have gone there. For some reason, he told me not too long ago, he's always had confidence in my ability to get along; he trusts me, as I do him. That seems to be the most important component of our relationship.

When I was twelve years old Buck moved to Tampa, Florida, and became a housing tract builder. I drove from Chicago that summer with my cousin Carl to visit him, and we were immediately put to work on a construction job. My uncle recently moved his office from the one he occupied in Tampa for twenty-five years. It's difficult for me to picture him in an office without the Atlantic sailfish he caught in 1952 on the wall over his head behind the desk, and the dusty, blue-backed copies of *Dutton's Navigation and Piloting* and *Advanced Celestial Navigation* on the shelf beside him.

Buck put my cousin and me to work in the desert north of town, a wasteland soon to be covered with cracker-box houses for the rapidly expanding population. The heat was unbearable: in the morning, when it was eighty-two degrees at eight o'clock, I felt beaten, trapped. There seemed to be no sky, only a hovering holocaust. I remember the foreman on the first job I worked for my uncle, a completely bald and eyebrowless man named Snood. He looked like a hairless gorilla.

The first day Snood drove me in his pickup truck out to the middle of nowhere and stopped, signaling me to get out and follow him. We walked over a rise in the sand until we came to a deep, narrow pit where a group of men were fitting together enormous sections of sewer pipe.

"This is a new boy," Snood yelled down to them. "He'll help you this morning." Snood then turned abruptly back to the truck, climbed in, and was gone. I looked back down at the men, none of whom seemed to take the slightest interest in me. I slid down the sandy slope into the ditch. Two of the men were struggling to keep a piece of pipe in place while four others attempted to attach another piece to it. I helped the men steady the section. When it was done, one of the men said to me, "I'm in for rape, how about you?"

All of the men laughed except one, the only black man on the job, who was digging shovelsful of sand out of the ditch and tossing them up over the edge.

"As you can see," said another of the men, "we poor peed-a-beds is tryin' to lay this cocksuckin' pipe in this goddamn ditch so some sonofabitchin' whore's ass can have hot water runnin' out her kitchen sink with a turn o' the same lily white wrist works her old man's joint. Ain't nothin' to it so long as you're as stupid and fucked up as the rest of us."

We worked for an hour or so before one of the men told me I could go take a drink if I wanted to. I climbed out of the ditch up to where an inverted trash can with a spigot sat on top of a card table under two of the skinniest and least shade-providing trees around. Next to the water can were two plastic cups, one red and one black. I filled the red one and drank it all in one gulp. Then I remembered my uncle's admonition about not drinking much water when you're hot and tired and short of breath so I only swallowed a small amount of a second cup, gargled the rest, and spit it out. Then I scrambled down into the ditch and went back to work.

"How come there are just two cups up there?" I asked one of the men.

"The red one's for the nigger," he said.

During the lunch break I lay down under the two skinny trees. At twelve-thirty Snood drove up and shouted to me to come over and hop into his truck, which I did. He drove me to another desert area but one within sight of a few houses. He drove slowly along a leveled stretch of yellow-green dirt.

"See that shit piled on the sides of the curbs?" he said. "That's lime rock." He stopped the truck and looked over at me. "Grab the shovel off the back and start shovelin' it off the curbs back into the street. We've got to shoot it tomorrow."

I got out and removed the shovel from the rear and watched Snood drive away. I looked around for a while then walked over to the curb and began shoveling. I had shoveled the lime rock completely off of one curb and had just begun working on the other when a steamroller came up the road, flattening the surface and forcing the excess lime rock back up onto the curb I had shoveled clean. The driver smiled as he went by and off down another newly begun road. I just stood there and stared at the lime rock covering the curb. It was a little disheartening so I went and sat down under a tree, one that was a bit more shade-providing than the ones where we had been laying sewer pipe, and fell asleep. By the time Snood returned I was awake and I ran over to the pickup, threw the shovel in the back, and got in. Snood didn't even look at the curbs. "Almost forgot about you," he chuckled.

Being the wealthiest state in the Deep South, Florida attracted a steady supply of transients, mostly from Alabama and Georgia, including a fair share of fugitives, men short on history and long on mean. Later, on a job building roads in Cocoa Beach, I watched a couple of lawmen pull up to the construction site in their beige-and-white, go up to an old boy I'd gotten to like pretty well, and haul him right off the steamroller he was driving without bothering to cut the ignition. Turned out he was a former Georgia sheriff wanted in that state for child molesting. He grinned and gave me the victory sign with his right hand as the law stuffed him into the back seat.

My uncle would always show up at the job site in his banged-up Cadillac convertible, which he used like a pickup truck. He'd jump down into a ditch and show everybody how to dig or hop up on a roof and demonstrate the proper way to set trusses as if nobody else had ever dug a ditch or set a truss before. Inevitably, as he was trying to drive away, Buck's car would get stuck in the mud or sand. He would scramble around in his trunk for tools or boards and the workers would have to help push him out. The amazing thing to me was that despite all of Buck's eccentricities and often unreasonable demands people enjoyed working with him. He was obviously slightly insane but his spirit was ingenuous.

Shortly after the revolution in Cuba, Buck took Pops, my grandfather, with him to see what the situation was like. While walking through a plaza in Havana a squad of Fidelistas surrounded them and arrested my uncle. At their headquarters they showed Buck a photograph of a general of Batista's for whom he was a dead—almost literally so—ringer. The only reason they hadn't shot him in the street was that they couldn't understand what he'd be doing walking along in broad daylight in the company of an old man. The general's picture was on the front page of that day's newspaper. The resemblance between the general and my uncle was indeed remarkable, and after he'd proven his identity Buck bought a dozen copies of the paper to take home. Pops told me that Buck also did some magic tricks for the soldiers and they gave him a box of Montecristo cigars, supposedly Castro's favorite.

When I was eighteen years old and traveling through Europe, I went into the Traveler's Aid office in the railroad station at Ghent, Belgium, to find out how to get to Zeveneken, the nearby town where a friend of mine lived. A man in the office who'd come in to check a train schedule told me he'd show me where to catch the bus and led me outside to the front of the station. He spoke English and showed me on the post at the stop that the next bus for Zeveneken was not due to leave for almost four hours. He said that his wife and child were due in at about the same time on a train from Antwerp. He looked me over carefully and asked if I was hungry. I told him I was. "Come on then," he said. "You can come home with me for a while and we will eat. Then I will drive you back here."

I was very hungry and decided to go along. He was a small man, in his forties, pasty-faced but with very dark eyes and hair. He spoke English with a strange accent, definitely not French or Flemish. "You're not from Belgium originally," I asked him, "are you?"

We were in his *deux chevaux*, trundling down a cobblestone street. Ghent looked to me like a storybook land. Even the rain had stopped, leaving everything glistening, immaculate. I was glad to be out of Paris.

"I am Russian, from Minsk," said my benefactor. "My name is Bulgakov." "Did you learn English in Russia?" I asked. "You speak perfectly." "I lived in the United States for fourteen years," he said. "I was a navigator on boats, first in the Gulf of Mexico, then on the Great Lakes. I lived for two years in Galveston, Texas, then for twelve years outside Chicago."

"I grew up partially in Chicago," I told Bulgakov. "Where did you live there?" "In Skokie," he said. "On Laramie Street." I laughed. "Really?" I said. "My uncle Buck lived for many years on Laramie Street in Skokie. He was in the construction business and built most of the houses in that part of town."

Bulgakov looked at me and half smiled. "Colby Construction Company, yes? Your uncle was Buck Colby?" "Yes!" I said. "Were you a neighbor of his? I used to spend a lot of time there." "My father and I bought a house from your uncle," said Bulgakov. "He was a good fellow. It was a good house." "That's amazing," I said. "Does your father still live there?" "No," said Bulgakov, "he is dead." "What a coincidence, though," I said, "your knowing my uncle Buck." I introduced myself and we shook hands as he drove. "Why did you come here?" I asked. "Are you still a navigator?" "No, I don't work on boats now. I am a stateless person, allowed to remain because my wife and son are Belgian citizens. My wife works and I take care of the boy and the house. Also, I am writing a book about what happened to me in America."

I was, of course, about to ask what had happened to him in America when Bulgakov pulled the car into the driveway of a modest but handsome two-story house on a short street. "This is a nice place," I said as we got out of the car. Bulgakov again gave me a half-smile. "We'll go in," he said. "I'll make you some dinner and I will tell you a story about your country." As I ate, or attempted to eat (there was too much for me) the wonderful meal Bulgakov prepared—steak, spinach, potatoes, salad, bread, cake—he told me how during the fifties, because he was Russian, he had been blacklisted as a Communist and prevented from working on ships in the United States.

"I was *not* a Communist," he said. "It was because of Stalin that my father and I left the Soviet Union and went to America. My mother and sister were murdered by the pig Stalin. America was *freedom*! We were good citizens. My father could not speak English, only a little. He was too old to learn, but I became a citizen, I studied hard, and then the government says I am a spy and I cannot work."

"Did they prosecute you?" I asked. "As a spy, I mean," "No. They *per*secuted me, made sure I could not get a job on a seagoing vessel anywhere in the country. The unions would do nothing for me, pretended I was dead. So much for the so-called 'commie' unions! Look, I'll show you something." Bulgakov went upstairs and returned a few minutes later, carrying a large box.

"These are the letters," Bulgakov said, pulling papers from the box. "Letters and documents from the ten years I spent clearing my name. I spent ten thousand dollars in legal fees to prove that I was not a Communist, to make the government allow me to work again on boats, to remove my name from the blacklist. It took all those years and all that money to accomplish this. My father died, not only from old age but shame and pain, knowing the accusations were false. We had to sell the house your uncle built so that we could have money to live. Nobody would hire me. I was a 'security risk.' Such shit it was. Finally I did it, I cleared my name, and when I did I left America and came here, first to Brussels, where I knew some people, then, after I married, to Ghent. I gave up my American passport, renounced my citizenship that I had studied so hard to earn. I am a free citizen now. I live here, I hope I will die here. Do you want more coffee?"

"No, no thank you," I said. "I can't eat anymore. That's a terrible story." "Yes, terrible," said Bulgakov. "But there are many worse stories, of course. Especially in the Soviet Union. That is the only place worse than the United States."

Bulgakov drove me back to the train station, where I met his wife, a pretty red-haired woman, and their two-year-old son. He told his wife that I was a "stray" from the U.S.A., that he'd given me a meal and allowed me to freshen up at their house. I felt bettter not only for having eaten but Bulgakov had also insisted that I take a bath and shave. I was extremely grateful for the hospitality, I told his wife, and would be glad to return the same if they came to America.

"Thank you but no," said Bulgakov, not smiling as he spoke. "My wife and son don't need that other kind of hospitality I was so priviledged to receive, the kind that is beyond your control." We took his wife and son to the car and then Bulgakov walked me to the bus stop. "So good-bye, my friend," Bulgakov said, shaking my hand. "Please do not thank me anymore. I want you to know I loved the United States, I loved my house your uncle built, it was a fine house. I am sorry but I will never see it again. I don't *have* to stay here. I *want* to. I am a free man. Good-bye."

We shook hands and Bulgakov walked back to his car. The bus to Zeveneken arrived and I got on. I took a window seat and looked back for Bulgakov. He was holding up his son and talking to him.

When I told my uncle about meeting Bulgakov, Buck remembered him, and he recalled that he'd actually sold the house to the elder Bulgakov. Buck knew that the son had had some difficulty with the government, but he thought it had been with the immigration service. My uncle didn't know the extent of Bulgakov's problem, however, and didn't know why he'd sold the house.

My main pastime with Uncle Buck has been fishing. He's always had a boat for us to go out on in the Gulf of Mexico and we've spent most of our time together that way. No expedition was a success, however—at least in Buck's estimation—unless there was an element of real danger involved. Buck and his second wife had almost been killed during a race across Lake Michigan when they were caught in a storm and the mast of Buck's sailboat broke in two, and in February of 1973 my uncle and I were almost killed aboard a boat we were sailing for a friend of his across the Gulf Stream, from Nassau to Coral Gables when a vicious squall came within a few feet of cracking us up on a breakwater off Miami. Before we left on that trip from the Bahamas I asked Uncle Buck when we'd be back in Tampa. "Who knows?" he said. "We may never get back."

Once when I was about fourteen we ran aground on a sandbar several miles out in the Gulf. Rather than wait the thirty minutes or so until the tide was due to change, Buck told me to get out of the boat and push. I dutifully jumped over the side and had begun to rock the boat in order to free it when I spotted a large dorsal fin heading straight for me. I immediately hoisted myself back into the boat and watched the fin glide by. "What are you doing?" asked my uncle. "Why aren't you in the water?" "Shark," I told him. "A big one just swam by." "Don't worry about the sharks," he said. "I'll tell you if I see one."

The last time Buck was in East Africa he packed himself a lunch one day and wandered off into the bush alone. At some point during his hike he was confronted on the trail by a large native who refused to or could not speak either English or Swahili, in which languages my uncle attempted to ingratiate himself. "He was a mean-looking guy and was carrying a big machete," Buck told me. "He wouldn't let me by." "What did you do?" I asked. "Turn around and go back?" "No," Buck laughed. "Of course not. I had a wonderful day; I walked for miles and saw all kinds of wild game." "What about the native?" I said. "How did you get past him?" "Oh, no problem," said Buck. "I just gave him my lunch."

In recent years Buck has developed a particular fondness for exceedingly primitive places. Now seventy years old, he's spent the greater part of the last few building a house, his "last resort" as he calls it, on the island of Utila, off the coast of Honduras directly north of La Ceiba and east of Monkey-River Town, Belize. The local population numbers approximately three thousand. There are power poles along the one main road of the island but as of yet no electrical lines. Power is provided several hours a day by a generator. Most of the inhabitants are descendants of pirates; the most common surnames are Morgan and Jones. It is a remittance island: since there is no industry all of the young adults leave as soon as they are able in order to find work, sending money home to relatives still on Utila. The waters around the island are shark-infested but the fishing is excellent. Gambling is legal in Honduras and there is an island bar where men and women play roulette and shoot craps in their bare feet while hens and roosters strut around among their legs on the floor. Prostitution is practiced openly. There is a town maniac, a sorcerer of whom everyone is afraid; every so often he has a fit and jumps around in the street shouting and screeching and threatening passersby with the evil eye. The feeling is of a frontier outpost, a barely civilized settlement where anything can happen, much as in the novels of Gabriel García Márquez, who writes of his nearby homeland, Colombia.

The big news these days in Honduras—as it is everywhere in Central America—is the revolution; the vying of the two government parties, the Reds and the Blues, both military groups who are presently fighting for the right to govern the country. Counterinsurgency groups are training in the mountains of mainland Honduras, from which they make forays into Guatemala to combat the Cuban-backed rebels. In the capital, Tegucigalpa, called "Tuh-goosey," dozens of left-wing soldiers have been abducted by masked gunmen, ostensibly secret police similar to Papa Doc's Tontons Macoute in Haiti. Former members of the ousted Nicaraguan National Guard and Salvadoran police on loan have set up death squads in order to frighten the liberals; however, the Lorenzo Zelaya Popular Revolutionary Command, a left-wing guerilla group, recently claimed credit for the shooting of two United States military advisers and the bombing of the Honduran Congress, marking, in their words, the start of an "armed struggle against the Yankee imperialism."

The people of Utila, the treasure hunters, impoverished fishermen, cayman-skinners, and others, cannot help but wonder what will happen to them if there is a successful revolution. Their island is isolated, with little to offer any government other than a location for a military outpost. Uncle Buck has built his house on a needle-tip peninsula, a strip of sand accessible by foot only at low tide. It's a beautiful structure, a roundhouse with twelve exterior doors and an exposed wood-beam ceiling. Concrete posts sunk twelve feet below the high-tide line support the house, making it the most well-built edifice on the island. I told my uncle that when the rebels take control they're going to make his house their command post on the island. "How many years do you think it'll be before they take over?" Buck asked me. "Four, five, tops," I said. "Well, that's all right," he said. "They can have it after that. I don't think I'll be much good to anybody after I'm seventy-five anyway."

Most of the island is still jungle and swamp; for transportation Buck rides around on a large Kawasaki motorcycle, and has rapidly become a well-known figure to the local citizenry. One afternoon Buck spotted a group of young boys looking like Bunuel's *Los Olvidados* dragging a dead python down the main street of the town. He went over to them and asked them how much they would be willing to sell it for. They couldn't name a price so my uncle offered them fifty cents and made the deal.

Buck took the python, which was about seven or eight feet long, and with his knife proceeded to skin it on the spot. He showed the boys, who may or may not already have known, the proper way to make the initial incision, slicing the underbelly, and how to then split it into two sections, peeling back the skins carefully so as to preserve them in one still-connected piece. Severing the head proved impossible without a machete, the python's vertebrae being almost as large as a man's, so after several minutes of futile hacking with the knife failed to dislodge it, Buck left the head attached. He took the severed hide and nailed it to a board, then sprinkled it liberally with salt. All of this he performed while in the middle of the main road, a large crowd having gathered around to observe the procedure. Nailed and salted, the python skin was placed on the roof of a friend's house, where it could dry unmolested.

When he was fifty Uncle Buck had skinned an alligator some cracker had shot on a pier on the Hillsborough River in Tampa. I was twelve years old then and I stood like the kids on the street in Honduras and watched him peel that gator for five hours in the sun. He let me carry the skin home, where we tacked it up on the side of the garage. I knew it was a five-hundred-dollar fine if he got caught with that alligator hide and I aked him if he worried about it being seen.

"People have to live," he said, "not worry. A man can't do both and expect to get away with anything."

When I reminded Buck, after he'd told me about the python, how I'd watched him skin the gator and what he'd said that day, he laughed and told me he'd been offered a hundred dollars for it by a county sheriff.

"He could have arrested me," said Buck, "but I just told him I couldn't let it go for less than three. Hell, it was hot out there on that pier."

I suppose the essence of my image of Uncle Buck is best reflected by his reaction to the disastrous tropical storm of 1975, when the worst hurricane in the history of the western hemisphere hit Central America, the hardest hit being Honduras. I hadn't heard from Uncle Buck for a while, and after reading the newspaper reports of the widespread death and destruction followed by famine and disease in his adopted republic, I was worried about him. A week after the hurricane I received a card postmarked La Ceiba. "Dear Nephew," it read. "Stories of Honduras highly exaggerated. Have seen only four dead, three bridges & roads out & killed two snakes trying to put oil in engine. Best, Uncle Buck."

The Gospel According to Chip Hilton

During the late fifties I discovered and read all of the Chip Hilton sports books by Clair Bee. The hero of *Touchdown Pass, Strike Three, Hoop Crazy, Pitchers' Duel, Dugout Jinx*, and twenty or more other titles, Chip Hilton, as invented by Bee, was a tall, handsome, blond-haired, gray-eyed boy in the small town of Valley Falls who was a great athlete and exemplary human being. There was nobody nicer or fairer or a more intense and dedicated athletic competitor than Chip, and I wanted to be just like him even though I had dark hair and blue eyes, wasn't particularly tall, lived in a big city, was not always nice or fair, and, even though I was a good athlete, was too often indifferrent to the outcome of games in which I was playing.

Clair Bee had been a famous basketball coach at Long Island University, and the Chip Hilton series stressed sportsmanship combined with an acute knowledge of baseball, basketball, and football. Each story involved Chip in dual sporting and social dilemmas that inevitably culminated in a tension-filled but ultimately satisfying climax.

There was never an unhappy ending. The overall title of Coach Bee's pantheon could just as well have been *The Gospel According to Chip Hilton.*

Chip lived with his mother, who was an operator at the Valley Falls telephone company. His father, "Big Chip," had been killed in an accident at the local pottery, where he had been foreman. My mother knew that I would have preferred her to be a little old gray-haired lady who worked at the phone company and did nothing else but keep house and care for me, and she used to tease me about it. She was a beautiful, sophisticated, relatively high-living young woman in those days, but I didn't really care because none of my friends' mothers were like Chip Hilton's mother either.

Since none of my friends were any more like Chip than I was, I had a difficult time believing that somebody like Chip could really exist. Even at twelve or thirteen years old it seemed too fantastic to me—especially since the still-reigning conception of Chicago boyhood was James T. Farrell's *Studs Lonigan* (which I was also reading in those days)—but I still read each new Hilton story as it appeared. I was actually kind of glad there was nobody in real life—*my* life—like him. It somehow made the books more exciting, and at that point I had no great interest in reality anyway.

Years later I found the first three Chip Hilton books selling for forty cents each in a used bookshop in New

Orleans. I bought them and reread the first, *Touchdown Pass*. Since it had been written in 1948 some of the football information was outdated, rules had changed, and certain strategies and formations were no longer employed, but the descriptions of the games still rang true, and though Chip was certainly as premier a do-gooder and as invincible an athlete as I remembered, I was astonished to discover just how right it all felt. There were good guys and bad guys and in-between guys, and though the story was a rather obvious morality lesson, it all seemed sensible without being overly righteous or hopelessly corny. I couldn't help thinking that if Somerset Maugham had written American boys' sports stories they would have been something on the order of the Chip Hilton books.

In *Touchdown Pass*, Chip manages to help a friend's father find a job and get it back after he's lost it unfairly, captain and quarterback his high school team to the state championship despite a broken leg, and keep the peace among warring teammates. All of this is accomplished while Chip holds down a part-time job as a storeroom clerk each evening and is an outstanding student during the day. Pretty Jack Armstrong-ish to be sure, but Clair Bee made Chip a bit different, he made him moody and often mistaken and even vain. That Chip was always able to overcome these lapses in character was certainly unreal, and rarely was a girl mentioned, but at least there was something real about him.

I imagine that I must have learned something from reading those books, and that I'm probably still operating according to some of those same principles and under those same delusions. What makes it possible to believe in something you know is impossible and to act as if it were not only possible but true? Maybe that's the only way anybody can ever really believe in anything.

The Getaway

Shortly after my father died, my mother sent me to live with my uncle Buck in Tampa, Florida. I was twelve and a half years old, and I drove from Chicago to Tampa with my cousin Carl, Uncle Buck's son, who was eighteen, a student at the University of Illinois. In Tampa, Uncle Buck put us to work on one of his construction projects, laying sewer pipe and shooting streets. Working construction in the extremely hot, humid Florida weather left Carl and me exhausted on weeknights; we always went to bed early so that we could be up before six the following morning to go to work.

Our social life, therefore, was limited to Saturdays and Sundays. On Saturday I usually went fishing with my uncle on his boat in the Gulf of Mexico. On one of these excursions I got terrible sun blisters on my face; huge, ugly, carbuncle-like welts, which Uncle Buck attempted to doctor. He used a pumice stone to rub my face raw, eliminating the blisters but also most of the skin on my cheeks. Not only was this radical treatment painful, but it left my face glowing bright red on either side of my nose. I walked with my friend Vinnie up to River Grove Pharmacy, where the druggist, Eduardo Pabros, applied a white salve and white powder to my wounds. Eduardo gave me a tube of the salve and a can of powder and told me to keep applying them until my face healed. He would charge them to my uncle's account, he said. "And next time," he told me, "go to a different doctor."

The next evening I went bowling with Vinnie, my cousin Carl, and several other boys. We stayed at the alley for three or four hours, and when we were finished Vinnie, who was my age, and I were changing out of the rented bowling shoes into our own when we noticed that the other boys, including Carl, had disappeared. They had all run out without paying. Since Vinnie and I had very little money and could not possibly pay the entire bill, we ran out, too.

Two or three days later, my aunt, who at that time was a serious bowler, participating in various leagues, asked me if I wanted to go bowling with her. I was taking a week off from work because Eduardo Pabros suggested that I stay out of the sun until my blisters healed. I told my aunt sure, I loved to bowl. To my surprise, we went to the same bowling alley the boys and I had gone to a few nights before. My aunt and I had been bowling for about thirty minutes when the manager, who apparently knew my aunt well, came up and started talking to her. He then came over to me and asked if I had been at the alley with a group of boys on the weekend who had run out without paying. "Of course not," I said. He recognized me, he said, because my face was painted white. He knew I'd been there with that bunch of deadbeat kids, he insisted, getting more animated now. "You seen any other kid around here with goo on his face?"

My aunt was mortified. She asked for and paid the bill we had run up, then we left the bowling alley. She didn't say much on our drive home, only that this was very embarrasing for her. She knew whose fault it was though—my cousin Carl's. Not only was he much older than the rest of the boys, but he was my uncle's son from a previous marrriage. I knew that my aunt disliked the fact that my uncle had been married before, and she had never treated Carl well, constantly making disparaging remarks about him in Uncle Buck's presence.

When we got back to the house my uncle was there and my aunt carried on about how his son Carl had instigated this caper. I was just a young kid, she said, who had been caught up in the event. Carl was almost nineteen, he should know better, he was irresponsible, he was a criminal. After she completed her tirade, my aunt stormed off to her bedroom. Carl was still at work. My uncle asked me what I thought of the situation.

"Gee, Unk," I said, "you know it's really kind of your fault."

"*My* fault?"

"Yeah. I mean, if you hadn't messed up my face like this, they never would have recognized me when I went back to the bowling alley."

The Deep Blue See

When I was in the eighth grade I was given the job of being one of the two outdoor messengers of Clinton School. Since I was far from being among the best behaved students, I could only surmise that some farsighted teacher (of whom there were very few) realized that I was well suited for that certain responsibility, that perhaps some of my excess energy might be put to use and I'd be honored and even eventually behave better because of this show of faith in my ability to run errands during school hours. Either that or they were just glad to get rid of me for a half hour or so.

I thought it was great just because it occasionally allowed me to get out of not only the classroom but the school. Escorting sick kids home was the most common duty but my favorite was walking the blind piano tuner across California Avenue to and from the bus stop.

For two weeks out of the year the old blind piano tuner used to come each day and tune all of the pianos in the school. My job during that time was to be at the bus stop at eight forty-five every morning to pick him up, and then, at whatever time in the afternoon he was ready to leave, to walk him back across, wait with him until the bus arrived, and help him board.

I became quite friendly over the two-week period that I assisted him. I was twelve years old and the piano tuner looked to me like any ordinary old guy with white hair in a frayed black overcoat, except he was blind and carried a cane. My dad and I had seen Van Johnson as a blind man in the movie *Twenty-three Paces to Baker Street.* Van Johnson had reduced an intruder to blindness by blanketing the windows and putting out the lights, trapping him—or her, as it turned out—until the cops came, but I'd never known anybody who was blind before.

I couldn't really imagine not being able to see and on the last day I asked the piano tuner if he could see anything at all. We were crossing the street and he looked up and said, "Oh yes, I see the blue. I can see the deep blue in the sky and the shadows of gray around the blue."

It was a bright sunny winter day and the sky was clear and very blue. I told him how blue it was, I didn't see any gray, and there were hardly any clouds. We were across the street and I could see the bus stopping a block away.

"Were you ever able to see?" I asked.

"Oh yes, shapes," he said. "I can see them move."

Then the bus came and I helped him up the steps and told the bus driver the old man was blind and to please wait until I'd helped him to a seat. After the piano tuner was seated I said good-bye, gave the token to the driver, and got off.

While I was waiting at the corner for the traffic to slow so that I could cross, I closed my eyes and tried to imagine what it was like to be blind. I looked up with my eyes closed. I couldn't see anything. I opened them up and ran across the street.

The Story of My Life

When I was twelve I played in an important game in Little League baseball. Whichever team won the game would be in the playoffs. My team wasn't very good, but somehow we'd managed to get to that point, and the team we were playing was the previous year's champions.

Harvey, a kid I had known and disliked since first grade, was pitching for them. He was a left-hander and he'd shut out our team through the first six innings—we played only seven-inning games. I had gotten the only hit off of him, a bunt single on a three and nothing count in the first inning. Harvey was afraid to let me hit. He knew I could hit him, and he'd tried to walk me in the first but I had surprised him by bunting and beaten it out. My next two times up, the catcher interfered by tipping my bat, giving me a free pass to first base. I knew he'd done it on purpose, to keep me from hitting against Harvey, and I was furious.

I was the star hitter of my team and I was expected to get us some runs, so it had been a particularly frustrating game. Harvey's team had three runs. It was the bottom of the seventh inning, our last chance, and I stole second base. Then I stole third. Unnerved, Harvey walked the next two batters.

He was afraid of losing his shutout now, not to mention the game. Even though there were two outs, I figured we had a good chance to score. Harvey was nervous and I kept taunting him from third base. Then I saw who was up: Alvie Weinstock, the worst hitter on the team, if not the worst hitter in the entire league. I couldn't believe it. The coach, in an apparent effort to be "fair," to give everyone a chance to play, had pinch-hit Weinstock for our pitcher, who was not a bad hitter. I knew why he'd done it, though: Alvie Weinstock's father was an assistant coach on our team.

I yelled at the coach, "Let Goodman hit! Let Goodman bat for himself!" But he wouldn't listen.

Before Weinstock knew what had happened, Harvey'd slipped two strikes across the plate. There was no doubt that Weinstock was going to strike out, we'd lose, it would be the end of the season, and hated Harvey would have pitched a one-hit shutout. It was all too much for me to take. I took a long lead off of third base.

"Hey, Harvey, hey, hey," I yelled.

Harvey looked over at me. All he had to do was throw one more pitch to Weinstock and it would be all over. I dared him to try and pick me off. I was counting on Harvey's vanity, and it worked—Harvey threw over to the third baseman, lazily, just to keep me close. I broke for home on the dead run.

Everybody was screaming. I yelled at Weinstock to block the catcher, to step in front of him, get in his way so that I could score. Instead, Weinstock stepped back, out of the box. The catcher, who was smart—remember he'd tipped my bat twice—and good, blocked the plate. I was out by ten feet.

All of the coaches stormed around me while I lay there. I wasn't anywhere near the plate.

Mr. Weinstock was yelling down at me. "You're incorrigible!" he shouted—he didn't like me anyway. "You're a delinquent!" He was louder than anyone.

"Alvie would have struck out," I said to him. "I wanted to break the shutout."

My stepfather was there. He'd come to pick me up after the game and had seen what had happened. Mr. Weinstock started yelling at him.

"Does he listen at home? He's no good, that kid, no good, I tell you. He doesn't follow orders. He's gonna end up no good."

My stepfather didn't like me much either, but he didn't give a damn about baseball, and he wasn't stupid—at least, not stupid enough to get carried away by a twelve-year-old's baseball game—so he didn't say anything. Then the coach came over.

"I'm not going to let you play in the All-Star game because of that stunt," he said to me, although he later relented because I was the only one on the team chosen to play and he wanted the team to be represented.

I began taking off my spikes, changing into my regular shoes. Harvey came over.

"Nice try," he said.

"Fuck you," I said.

Then my stepfather and I drove home.

"How was the game?" my mother asked.

When I didn't say anything she looked at my stepfather for an answer.

"They lost," he told her.

"Oh, that's too bad. You must be disappointed," she said to me.

"Yes," I said.

"Well then," she said, "I'll leave you alone."

I thanked her and went into my room.

"He's so sensitive," I heard her say to my stepfather before I closed the door.

The Kid Who Torched
the *Charterhouse of Parma*

Green Briar Park, bounded by Peterson, Washtenaw, Talman, and Glenlake Streets, consisted of a baseball and football field (sans goalposts) encircled by magnificent Dutch elm trees, a concrete outdoor basketball court with chain-net baskets, and a field house.

There were baseball games at GB, as the park was called, every clear day from April until the first snow. We played softball only, not hardball, with a sixteen-inch "Clincher" and no gloves. Balls hit into the overhanging trees were usually playable if caught—if the tree interfered with a player's catching a ball and it dropped to the ground, it was considered a foul ball; if it was caught before hitting the ground, the batter was out.

Kids of all ages played ball at GB, even guys who'd graduated or dropped out of high school. One famous regular was Chuck Syracuse, a crazy kid who'd been thrown out of school at the age of nineteen, in his third year of high school, and spent every day at GB playing softball. At night he drove a cab. He always carried around with him big, important-looking books, like the *Charterhouse of Parma* and the *Brothers Karamazov*. My guess is that Syracuse never attempted to read these books; he just wanted us to think that he did. There was a pile of them on the back floor of his cab, so I imagine every once in a while a customer perused one or two.

One afternoon Syracuse came by in his cab, got out to watch the game for a few minutes—he needed extra money, he said, so that week he was working days, too—and after an inning or so somebody left and Chuck took his place. It was a high-scoring game that went into extra innings, it took a long time to play, and when Syracuse got back to his taxi he discovered that he'd left the meter running. He went berserk and began beating on the roof of the cab. Finally he got in and drove away.

A few days later—during which time Chuck had not shown up at GB—we found out that Syracuse had turned the cab over in an empty lot in another neighborhood and torched it (and, presumably, the books, too), then told the cab company that it had been stolen while he was eating lunch. The company didn't buy his story and investigated the case. When they confronted him with the truth, he told them he'd done it so that he wouldn't be charged the thirty-five bucks run up on the meter while he'd been playing soft-ball at the park.

Since Chuck couldn't pay the three or four grand the company said he owed them for the cab, he did a little time at Joliet. After he got out of the joint Chuck continued to hang out at GB, where he suddenly found himself a famous person. He spent more time answering questions about his insane torch job than playing softball. One day Magic Frank was kidding around and asked Syracuse if he thought he'd handled the situation properly.

"What do you mean?" Chuck asked.

"Do you think it was worth it?" said Frank.

"Well," said Syracuse, thinking it over a bit, "you know I went four for five in the game that day."

The Chinaman

I always spotted the Chinaman right off. He would be at the number two table playing nine ball with the Pole. Through the blue haze of Bebop's Pool Hall I could watch him massé the six into the far corner.

My buddy Magic Frank and I were regulars at Bebop's. Almost every day after school we hitched down Howard to Paulina and walked half a block past the Villa Girgenti and up the two flights of rickety stairs next to Talbot's Bar-B-Q. Bebop had once driven a school bus but had been fired for shooting craps with the kids. After that he bought the pool hall and had somebody hand out flyers at the school announcing the opening.

Bebop always wore a crumpled Cubs cap over his long, greasy hair. With his big beaky nose, heavy-lidded eyes, and slow, half-goofy, half-menacing way of speaking, especially to strangers, he resembled the maniacs portrayed in the movies by Timothy Carey. Bebop wasn't supposed to allow kids in the place, but I was the only one in there who followed the Cubs, and since Bebop was a fanatic Cub fan, he liked to have me around to complain about the team with.

The Chinaman always wore a gray fedora and sharkskin suit. Frank and I waited by the Coke machine for him to beat the Pole. The Pole always lost at nine ball. He liked to play one-pocket but none of the regulars would play anything but straight pool or nine ball or rotation. Sometimes the Pole would hit on a tourist for a game of eight ball but even then he'd usually lose, so Frank and I knew it wouldn't be long before we could approach the Chinaman.

When the Chinaman finished off the Pole he racked his cue, stuck the Pole's fin in his pocket, lit a cigarette, and walked to the head. Frank followed him in and put a dollar bill on the shelf under where there had once been a mirror and walked out again and stood by the door. When the Chinaman came out, Frank went back in.

I followed Frank past Bebop's counter down the stairs and into the parking lot next to the Villa Girgenti. We kicked some grimy snow out of the way and squatted down and lit up, then leaned back against the garage door as we smoked.

When we went back into the pool hall Bebop was on the phone, scratching furiously under the back of his Cub cap while threatening to kick somebody's head in, an easy thing to do over the phone. The Chinaman was sitting against the wall watching the Pole lose at eight ball. As we passed him on our way to the number nine table he nodded without moving his eyes.

"He's pretty cool," I said.

"He has to be," said Frank. "He's a Chinaman."

Big Steve, King Levinsky, & Other Real Americans I Have Known

The only one of my friends who remembers my dad is Big Steve. Steve has been interested in history and current events ever since I've known him, and that's forty years now. We grew up together in Chicago and always have been close friends. When we were about ten, the Mohawk gas station on the corner of Rockwell Street and Devon Avenue was giving away drinking glasses with pictures of all the presidents of the United States on them; underneath each president's picture were the dates of his term in office. I remember that Steve made his father buy gas at the Mohawk station just so he could get the set of six with a fill-up. Steve studied a glass at every meal, memorizing the presidents' names and dates of tenure. "John Quincy Adams," he'd say to me as we walked together to school, "1825 to 1829." A half-block farther on he'd say, "Zachary Taylor, 1849 to 1850. Died in office." And so on. That's how Big Steve learned the presidents.

For several years he was an executive producer for network television news, and we saw each other when Steve came out to San Francisco to cover the 1984 Democratic National Convention. More than a few people we knew in the old days might be just a little surprised that Big Steve made good. One of them would certainly be Peter Miscinski, one of our high school history teachers. Miscinski hated Big Steve because Steve was a class clown, a joker who loved to poke fun at him. Miscinski was an easy target, though, and was hardly a match for Steve's witty and often caustic remarks. Big Steve brought a pillow with him to class one day, put it on his desk, and laid his head down. Miscinski came charging over and asked Steve just what he thought he was doing. "You put me to sleep every day," Big Steve told him, "so I'm just making myself more comfortable."

Another time Miscinski really thought he had Steve in big trouble. He'd seen Steve in school earlier in the day and when history class began Steve was absent. Cutting a class meant automatic early morning penalty hours and Miscinski knew how much Steve hated getting up early, so he was grinning widely as he began calling the class roll. As Miscinski got to the *B*'s—Big Steve's last name begins with an *F*—I saw the classroom door open and then close. Through the legs of the kids seated in the first row, I spied Steve crawling on his knees down the aisle toward the back of the room. Miscinski hadn't seen the door open and close. Those of us who had, however, and who watched as Steve stealthily made his way as silently and unobtrusively as possible toward his seat, did our best to stifle our laughter.

Just as Miscinski got to Steve's name on the roll and called it out, pen poised to mark absent, Steve reached his seat, raised himself into it, and said in a loud voice, "Present, sir!" Miscinski slammed his attendance book down on his desk, his jaw dropped, his glasses fell off. "But you're not!" Miscinski yelled. "*You're* not here!" Big Steve just grinned at Miscinski while everyone in the room roared with laughter. Big Steve had done it again.

The ironic thing is that Steve really did like both Miscinski and the study of modern history. He just couldn't help clowning around. Now he's in the Big Time, and with all that advertising money at stake he can't afford to fool around quite as much. Big Steve hasn't lost his sense of humor, however. The day before he was to leave New York for San Francisco we were talking on the telephone and I asked him, "What days do you want to go to the convention?" Steve just laughed and said, "None. We'll watch it on television."

Regarding politicians, Big Steve's point of view isn't too far removed from what King Levinsky, the former heavyweight fighter, remarked to my father in my presence in about 1954. "Dem guys," the King told my dad, "ain't none of 'em on da square. Dey can't be," said the King, "it's part of da job." King Levinsky, of course, was, like Big Steve, a Chicago boy. He gained a certain amount of notoriety by being knocked out on August 8, 1935, by Joe Louis. When I knew him I was a small boy and the King was selling hand-painted ties around the swimming pools of the luxury hotels on Miami Beach. According to the sports writer Ira Berkow—also a Chicago guy—the King claimed that Frank Sinatra once paid him a C-note for one of his ties; Al Capone, another of Levinsky's customers, donated fifty. The King was reputed to have made nearly a half-million dollars during his ring career, but he wound up punch-drunk and broke. What happened to the money? "Bad managers," said the King. "Dey're de only ones rottener den da pols."

As it turned out, Big Steve and I did attend the convention together. We went on Tuesday, the evening Jesse Jackson was scheduled to speak, figuring that it would be the most emotionally charged moment of a generally dull event. The overwhelming feeling of a political convention these days—for a so-called "objective" observer, that is—is staleness. Due to the proliferation of primaries, the most important issue—the choosing of a presidential candidate—is already decided, thereby relieving the affair of any genuine tension. Big Steve and I agreed that perhaps the last truly interesting political convention had been in 1960, when John F. Kennedy won the Democratic nomination.

While we waited through Speaker of the House Tip O'Neill's speech, and then the lineup of Rainbow Coalition members who introduced Jesse Jackson, Big Steve and I discussed what some previous presidents and presidential candidates might have done with their lives had it not been for several fortuitous twists of fate. Gerald Ford, for example, is easy to imagine as a tire-store owner in Kalamazoo, Michigan. "Friendly Gerry" would have been great doing ads on local TV, a guy you could depend on to suggest the right tires for your car, to guarantee the work. Friendly Gerry wouldn't have tackled anything too mentally strenuous; he would be conservative, but fair-minded, a responsible member of the community. Hubert Humphrey could have been the neighborhood druggist, taking over the pharmacy from his dad, a guy who wouldn't overcharge you for prescriptions. As vice president, Humphrey had been obviously bent out of character when he backed LBJ all the way in the war in Vietnam. "And it came from the gut," Big Steve said to me. "He really believed in it."

Jackson's speech was a good one, he didn't hit a false note. He knew he had to be conciliatory and soft-pedal it or his career as a national politician would suffer. Jackson has modeled his machine after one of the best, Mayor Daley's, from the time of Martin Luther King's Operation Breadbasket, and he knows what it takes to survive. "Jesse looks like a stalking horse," Steve said. "He probably can't ever win, but he can clear the way for a more acceptable black candidate."

Watching Jackson gesticulate on the podium I remembered a night at a Golden State Warriors game in the Oakland Coliseum a couple of years before. The Warriors came running out and got a big hand—this is when they still had Bernard King and World B. Free on the team—and then a few minutes later, while the Warriors were shooting around, warming up, Jesse Jackson and a companion entered the arena and walked to their seats in the front row. The applause he received was deafening, much larger than that accorded the Warriors, and Jackson stood and waved to the crowd. A guy sitting behind me turned to the man next to him and asked, "Who does *he* play for?"

NBC commentator Tom Brokaw reported that as Jackson came off the podium following his speech he asked one of his aides, "How did the Jewish thing go over?" (A reference to an attempt to reconcile his recently having called New York "Hymie-town.") By that time Big Steve and I were on our way out of the Moscone Center. We'd sat through all but the final fifteen minutes or so of Jackson's speech in seats facing the podium, and then we went down to the NBC control booth to view the denouement. With forty pictures to choose from, the producers focused almost exclusively on people crying, holding children, those faces reflecting awe and rapture. These were, of course, genuine responses, but by no means did they represent the majority of the audience; they were, quite simply, the most sensational at the moment.

It felt good to get out into the cool night air of San Francisco. As Big Steve and I walked up Fourth Street toward Market, I recalled a definition of the word "democratic" I'd read earlier in the day in *Webster's New Collegiate*

Dictionary: "Favoring social equality; not snobbish or socially exclusive." Earlier, before going to the control booth, Steve and I had attempted to enter a "hospitality" room in the NBC offices at the convention center to watch part of Jesse Jackson's speech on television, but we had been turned away. "Sorry," the guard at the door told us, "this isn't for NBC people—this is for government people." From the doorway I could see Jackson's sweaty face on TV and hear him speaking about breaking down the barriers between classes. Most of the "government people" had their backs turned to the television set and were nibbling on prawns or pieces of cake.

Once, sometime in the forties, King Levinsky was arrested for attempting to pick a guy's pocket at the bar of the Hotel Maryland in Chicago, a popular watering hole for visiting firemen just down the street from my dad's place. "You can't do this to me!" the King shouted at the cops as they took him away. "I'm a real American!" I've never been able to figure out exactly what he meant by that.

Speakeasy

My actual introduction to the liquor business came not via my dad but through a guy about ten years older than I was named Arnie Farraday. Arnie was from Tupelo, Mississippi, and worked a regular job as a grave digger. His claim to fame, although it was never Arnie who spoke of it, was that he had once killed a man with one punch.

When I was first told this it seemed to me an incredible story, seeing as how Arnie was only five foot five inches tall and was, as far as I could tell, an extraordinarily even-tempered person. What had indeed happened was that while Arnie was in the army his wife had divorced him and married another man. This hurt Arnie terribly; he loved his wife very much, as well as their three-year-old daughter. One day in the barracks Arnie was showing a few of his buddies pictures of his wife and daughter when a drunken soldier stumbled in, pointed to the photograph of Arnies's ex-wife, and said, "Who's that whore?" Arnie hit him once in the face, knocking the soldier backward across the bunk. When he fell he hit his head on the railing and died. Arnie was given a general discharge.

He and I worked together for a while delivering liquor to "colored speakeasies," as Arnie called them, in Evanston, just across the Chicago line. Evanston is a dry town, and the speaks ordered their booze from the Howard Street taverns. We once delivered a dozen cases of Scotch during a snowstorm on Christmas Eve. We had to carry the cases down a narrow gangway to the back of an old wooden house, then down a long flight of precipitous, icy steps to the door, or rather doors—there was an outside screen door, then a wooden one, then a thick, soundproof door which opened into a large, dark cellar through which Arnie and I carried the cases; then up some stairs into an enormous kitchen where several girls sat around a table in slips and housecoats playing cards.

The proprietress, a heavyset middle-aged black woman with pince-nez hanging down her bosom, thanked us, and told us where to set the cases. She gave us each a glass of eggnog generously spiked with bourbon, and smiled at us, displaying at least five shiny gold teeth on the left side of her mouth. Having been there before, Arnie kidded around with the woman, whose name was Williestine, while I watched the girls. I was sixteen and had never been in a whorehouse before. All of the girls were different shades of brown, none of them were black. I thought they were the most interesting and beautiful women I had ever seen. Williestine, however, caught me looking and snapped, "These ain't your kind, honey. These for Easter rabbits," she said. "Chocolate bunnies. You dig?"

I was embarrassed and put down my drink. Williestine laughed but I could tell that for some reason she was really annoyed with me. I stood looking out the kitchen window at the blowing white flakes while Arnie finished his eggnog and bourbon. Nat Cole was singing "The Christmas Song" on the radio. Finally Arnie grinned his handsome, little boy's face at Williestine, joked a bit more, and said good-bye, having me precede him down the stairs and out the back door.

"What was she so upset about?" I asked Arnie when we were outside.

"Oh, she was just jealous you were paying so much attention to the girls," drawled Arnie, "instead of to her. My, my," he said, and laughed, as we made our way through the snow to the car, "that Williestine sure do have her pride."

Buddies

My old friend Moe called me up this afternoon from Chicago just to say hello. I hadn't seen or talked to him for almost two years, since the last time I was in Chicago, so it was a nice surprise. Moe is an automobile mechanic, he runs his own little garage up on North Clark Street near the lake. He still looks and sounds like he did twenty years ago, like a less-sensitive, more powerfully built James Dean, the same smile and coloring, with a high-pitched, almost girlish voice. I've always thought of Moe as the kind of guy my dad would have liked, that he would have picked up right away on Moe's inherent honesty and respected his ability to get things done.

Moe helped me to buy my first motorcycle—a Triumph—and my first car, a maroon 1955 Buick Century. When I first met Moe, who is six years older than I am, he was twenty-one and had the reputation of being one of the best wheel men in the city of Chicago. He'd recently been discharged from the service after a botched surgical procedure had left him scarred for life with a hideous circular burnlike scar on his right biceps.

Moe had been forced to join the army after he and a buddy, Davey Floyd, had gotten drunk on moonshine in Paris, Tennessee, Davey's hometown, then broken into the

Cadillac agency on Main Street, hot-wired an Eldorado, and driven straight out through the showroom's plate-glass window. The cops caught them only after Moe had run three roadblocks and the Eldorado had run out of gas. Moe had done time previously at St. Charles Reformatory outside Chicago, as a juvenile for car theft, so when the judge in Tennessee gave him a choice between the army or jail—a common practice in southern courts in the fifties—Moe did not hesitate to choose enlistment, as did Davey.

My cousin Chris introduced me to Moe, they were friends, and Moe immediately took me under his wing. I began hanging out with them and their gang, all of whom were in their twenties or older, when I was fifteen. They introduced me to motorcycles, grain alcohol, older women, and various other pastimes attractive to a healthy, reasonably curious midwestern adolescent. One time Moe bought a machine gun down on Maxwell Street for eighty dollars and came by my house to show it to me. I remember my mother calling me in for dinner while Moe and I stood on the sidewalk by the open trunk of his '57 Chrysler New Yorker as he pieced together the tommy gun.

Not long after I graduated from high school I began traveling, and did not return to Chicago for seven or eight years. When I finally did I called Moe, who was working out of the garage behind his mother's house, and he told me to come right over. When I got there Moe threw me a set of car keys, said, "Hi, man, follow me," and motioned for me to get into a huge Cadillac convertible. He climbed into a Ford van and drove off. I started up the Caddy and tailed him. Moe drove up and down streets I'd never seen before, stopping about twenty minutes later in an alley. He jumped out of the van, signaled for me to wait, and he ran through a gangway into the back of a house. In ten minutes he came out, hopped back into the van, pulled away. I followed him for another twenty minutes or so until he parked in front of a house on a quiet street in Evanston. Moe went into the house and came out five minutes later, opened the door on the driver's side of the Cadillac, motioned for me to shove over, which I did, slid behind the wheel, cranked the ignition, peeled away from the curb, and said, "Hey, man, great to see you. Where've you been?"

Moe never explained why he'd just had me follow him all over town and I never asked. I understood that he trusted me, that was enough. If I showed that I couldn't handle it he wouldn't ask me to do anything again. I knew if that ever happened Moe wouldn't make a big deal of it, there just would never be another opportunity for me to prove myself. I knew then, too, as I know now, that if I had to I could trust Moe with my life.

Moe was always a great mechanic. He knew I was different, that my ambitions weren't the same as his, and perhaps because of that we got along well. After I began to write and my books were published, Moe made an effort to show his confidence in me that way, too, by buying the books. When I told him that I'd be happy to give him copies, he said, "No man, you're the author. You write, the public buys. I'm the public." I appreciated this, coming from Moe, knowing that he'd read about six books in his life, all of them having to do with rebuilding automobile or airplane engines.

This afternoon on the phone Moe told me he'd been in New Jersey recently on a vacation with his girlfriend and had spotted a double-decker Greyhound Scenicruiser sitting in a yard just off the highway. It was raining that day, he said, and he pulled off the road and went over to have a look at the bus. As he was walking around looking it over a guy came out of a house and asked Moe if he could help him. Moe asked if the guy owned the bus and if it was for sale. The guy answered yes on both counts and Moe asked him how much. "Thirty-five hundred," said the guy. "Thirty-five hundred!" Moe said to me on the phone. "Jesus, I thought, the goddamn engine alone was worth more than that. It had a big Detroit diesel in there. So I gave him a thousand bucks and a bogus check for twenty-five hundred on the spot. I worked on it for a couple of days and then drove it back to Chicago. My girlfriend drove the car."

"How could you work on it," I asked Moe, "without your tools?"

"Hey, man, you know me," said Moe. "All I need is a wrench, pliers, and a screwdriver and I can make anything go." He explained that he was running a shuttle service with the bus between Chicago and the Wisconsin resorts. "I'm thinking of operating my own personal service with it down to Disney World in Orlando," Moe told me.

Since I live in California now I don't often get to see Moe, but the last time I did, two years ago in Chicago, I was staying at a ritzy hotel on the Near North Side. Moe came over to see me and we had a few beers in my room before going out to dinner. When we came out of the hotel there was one of Moe's inevitable Cadillac convertibles sitting at the curb right in front. The doorman, who obviously had been going crazy trying to decide whether or not to call a tow truck for the hour and a half Moe's Cadillac had been parked there, not knowing what to do about a late-model fire engine–red Eldorado with no license plates or city sticker that might possibly belong to some Syndicate bigshot, just stared at us as we got in and drove away.

As soon as Moe had maneuvered the Cad across Michigan Avenue and onto the Outer Drive, where he could let his souped-up V-8 loose, he turned to me and said, "Life's full of problems, man, that's just the way things are. But every so often we do have some fun, don't we?" Then Moe grinned like James Dean and gave it the gun.

The End of Racism

One of my favorite places to go when I was a kid in Chicago was Riverview, the giant amusement park on the North Side. Riverview, which during the fifties was nicknamed Polio Park, after the reigning communicable disease of the decade, had dozens of rides, including some of the fastest, most terrifying roller coasters ever designed. Among them were the Silver Streak, the Comet, the Wild Mouse, the Flying Turns, and the Bobs. Of these, the Flying Turns, a seatless ride that lasted all of thirty seconds or so and required the passengers in each car to recline consecutively on one another, was my favorite. The Turns did not operate on tracks but rather on a steeply banked, bobsledlike series of tortuous sliding curves that never failed to engender in me the sensation of being about to catapult out of the car over the stand of trees to the west of the parking lot. To a fairly manic kid, which I was, this was a big thrill, and I must have ridden the Flying Turns hundreds of times between the ages of seven and sixteen.

The Bobs, however, was the most frightening roller coaster in the park. Each year several people were injured or killed on that ride; usually when a kid attempted to prove his bravery by standing up in the car at the apex of the first long, slow climb, and was then flipped out of the car as it jerked suddenly downward at about a hundred miles per hour. The kids liked to speculate about how many lives the Bobs had taken over the years. I knew only one kid, Earl Weyerholz, who claimed to have stood up in his car at the top of the first hill more than once and lived to tell about it. I never doubted Earl Weyerholz because I once saw him put his arm up to the biceps into an aquarium containing two piranhas just to recover a quarter Bobby DiMarco had thrown into it and dared Earl to go after. Earl was eleven then. He died in 1958, at the age of fourteen, from the more than two hundred bee stings he sustained that year at summer camp in Wisconsin. How or why he got stung so often was never explained to me. I just assumed somebody had dared him to stick his arms into a few hives for a dollar or something.

Shoot the Chutes was also a popular Riverview ride. Passengers rode on boats that slid at terrific speeds into a pool and everybody got soaking wet. The Chutes never really appealed very much to me, though; I never saw the point of getting wet for no good reason. The Parachute was another one that did not thrill me. Being dropped to the ground from a great height while seated on a thin wooden plank with only a narrow metal bar to hold on to was not my idea of a good time. In fact, just the thought of it scared the hell out of me; I didn't even like to watch people do it. I don't think my not wanting to go on the Parachute meant that I was acrophobic, however, because I was extremely adept at scaling garage roofs by the drainpipes in the alleys and jumping from one roof to the next. The Parachute just seemed like a crazy thing to submit oneself to as did the Rotor, a circular contraption that spun around so fast that when the floor was removed riders were plastered to the walls by centrifugal force. Both the Parachute and the Rotor always had long lines of people waiting to be exquisitely tortured.

What my friends and I were most fond of at Riverview was Dunk the Nigger. At least that's what we called the concession where by throwing a baseball at a target on a handle and hitting it square you could cause the seat lever in the attached cage to release and plunge the man sitting on the perch into a tank of about five feet of water. All of the guys who worked in the cages were black, and they hated to see us coming. Between the ages of thirteen and sixteen my friends and I terrorized these guys. They were supposed to taunt the thrower, make fun of him or her, and try to keep them spending quarters for three balls. Most people who played this game were lucky to hit the target hard enough to dunk the clown one in every six tries; but my buddies and I became experts. We'd buy about ten dollars worth of baseballs and keep those guys going down, time after time.

Of course they hated us with a passion. "Don't you little motherfuckers have somewhere else to go?" they'd yell. "Goddamn motherfuckin' whiteboy, I'm gon' get yo' ass when I gets my break!" We'd just laugh and keep pegging hardballs at the trip-lever targets. My pal Big Steve was great at Dunk the Nigger; he was our true ace because he threw the hardest and his arm never got tired. "You fat ofay sumbitch!" one of the black guys would shout at Big Steve as he dunked him for the fifth pitch in a row. "Stop complaining," Steve would yell back at him. "You're getting a free bath, aren't ya?"

None of us thought too much about the fact that the job of taunt-and-dunk was about half a cut above being a carnival geek and a full cut below working at a car wash. It never occurred to us, more than a quarter of a century ago, why it was all of the guys on the perches were black, or that we were racists. Unwitting racists, perhaps; after all, we were kids, ignorant and foolish products of White Chicago during the fifties.

One summer afternoon in 1963, the year I turned sixteen, my friends and I arrived at Riverview and headed straight for Dunk the Nigger. We were shocked to see a white guy sitting on a perch in one of the cages. Nobody said anything but we all stared at him. Big Steve bought some balls and began hurling them at one of the black guys' targets. "What's the matter, gray?" the guy shouted at Steve. "Don't want to pick on one of your own?"

I don't remember whether or not I bought any balls that day, but I do know it was the last time I went to the concession. In fact, that was one of the last times I patronized Riverview, since I left Chicago early the following year and Riverview was torn down not long after. I don't know what Big Steve or any of my other old friends who played Dunk the Nigger with me think about it now, or even if they've ever thought about it at all. That's just the way things were.

The Favorite

It was my mother who introduced me to horse racing. She loved going to the track and often took me with her when I was a little boy. In Florida, at Hialeah, I loved to watch the pink flamingos pick their way among the fluttering green and yellow palms; and in Chicago, at Arlington Park or Sportsman's or Maywood, to listen to the heavyset, well-dressed men with diamond pinkie rings and ruler-length Havana cigars as they fussed over my mother, asking if she'd like something to eat or drink or if she wanted them to place a bet for her.

My father rarely, if ever, went to the racetrack. There may have been a bookmaking operation in the basement of his liquor store, but he told me that he didn't bet on anything with more than two legs that couldn't speak English. I doubt seriously if he'd ever heard of Xanthos, one of the two immortal horses of Achilles (the other being Balius) who had the power of speech and prophesied his master's death. If he had, I'm certain it would have served only to disaffect him further.

When I was in high school I became a real devotee of the so-called sport of kings. My friend Big Steve and I would often head for the track as soon as classes let out. Big Steve was a canny and gutsy bettor who won more often than he lost. Such was not the same in my case. I had as many off days as on and I always felt fortunate when I broke even. But there came a day I knew I couldn't lose. I was sixteen and Gun Bow, with Walter Blum up, was running in the feature race at A.P. I was certain there were no other horses in the eighth race that day that could beat Gun Bow, who was destined to be named Horse of the Year, beating out the great Kelso, a four-time winner of the award. The one problem for me was that I was broke at the time, so I had to borrow what I could in order to bet.

Big Steve was generous and loaned me twenty bucks. He was going through one of his periodic phases of gambling abstinence. Steve decided that he'd been gambling too much of late—horses, cards, craps—and he would test his willpower by refusing to bet on Gun Bow, even though he agreed with me that it was as close to a sure thing as there could possibly be. He even offered to drive me to the track and stand by me during the race.

Now, there are sure things and there are sure things. Gun Bow belonged in the former category. An example of the latter was the time my friend D.A. and I stopped before the first race to visit his uncle, Ralphie Love, who was working one of the ten-dollar combination windows in the clubhouse. Ralphie was a self-described "semiretired businessman" who formerly had been in the vending machine business. He now worked part-time at the track and spent a lot of time attending sports events. I used to see him regularly at college basketball games in Chicago in the early sixties, especially before the game-fixing, point-shaving scandal hit. The day D.A. and I saw him at the track Ralphie told us he thought the five horse, Count Rose, would be a nice bet in the first race. The jockeys liked him, Ralphie Love said. D.A. and I bet the five to win, he went off at nine to two, and sure enough, just as the pack hit the top of the stretch they parted like the Red Sea and Count Rose came pounding down the middle to win by a comfortable margin. What I didn't know about Gun Bow was whether or not the jockeys liked him.

I borrowed a total of a hundred dollars and Big Steve and I headed out toward Arlington Heights. I intended to bet only the eighth, no other races, so we didn't have to be there until around three o'clock. Post time would be at approximately three-thirty. I'd place my bet, watch them run, cash in, go home. The sun was out, the road uncrowded. As Big Steve and I rolled along in his dusty red Olds a warm feeling of well-being engulfed me. I was so confident that Gun Bow would win in a breeze that I told Big Steve I was going to put the entire C-note on the nose, not across the board as I'd originally planned.

When we were about ten minutes from the track, the sky suddenly clouded over. Then a few drops of rain appeared on the windshield. Thunder rolled, lightning flashed. Seconds later we were inundated by a torrential downpour. Big Steve turned on the windshield wipers full speed but it didn't do much good. It was one of those sudden blinding midwestern summer rainstorms. "Oh no," I said. "I can't believe this." "Don't worry," said Big Steve, "we'll make it on time." "That's not what I'm worried about," I said, "it's Gun Bow. How does he run in the mud?"

I worried the rest of the way to the racetrack. By the time we pulled into the parking lot the rain had slowed to a steady drizzle but I knew the track surface would no longer be fast and I had no idea what effect sloppy footing would have on Gun Bow's performance. Due to the storm we arrived later than we'd figured to and I had to make a dash for the betting window.

I met Big Steve at the rail near the finish line. The rain had stopped entirely. "So," he said, "what did you do?" I showed him the two fifty-dollar win tickets. There were puddles on the track. The starter's bell rang and the horses were off. I recalled the time I'd picked a long shot named Miss Windway out of the paper one morning before Big Steve, his brother Big Lar, and I went out to the track. I knew Miss Windway would win but by the time the seventh race, the one in which she was entered, rolled around, I was busted and had no more money to bet. I was disgusted with myself for having lost everything so quickly that day and didn't even bother to ask Steve or his brother for a loan. Big Steve, however, put six dollars across the board on Miss

Windway, Big Lar put two on the nose, and she went off at something like eighty-five to one. Miss Windway won the race by five lengths.

Now, I figured, even though I had to bet more money to win less, it was my turn. Gun Bow wouldn't let me down, he was too good a horse to let a little mud bother him. Walter Blum was a top jock, too; he wouldn't blow a big stakes race like this. As the horses were moving into the far turn a guy behind us shouted, "Do your job, Blum! I brought my gun with me today!" I turned away and looked up at the sky. The sun came out. As the horses reached the stretch an old guy next to me yelled, "Wa Wa Cy! Come on, Wa Wa Cy!" The odds on Wa Wa Cy, I knew, were fifteen to one. I looked at the man. The top of his head was bald and he was pulling hard with both hands at the small amount of hair he had left above his ears. At the wire Gun Bow was in front by three lengths.

On our way home Big Steve asked me what was the matter. Why was I so quiet? I'd won, hadn't I? "Just thinking," I said. In my mind I kept seeing that old guy tearing at his hair. "I don't think I'll ever really be much of a gambler," I told Big Steve. "It's foolish to bet long shots and no fun to bet the favorite." Steve laughed. "You didn't see *me* betting," he said, "did you?" The sky clouded over again and I closed my eyes. Wa Wa Cy, I thought, how could that guy have bet on Wa Wa Cy?

No More Mr. Nice Guy

My buddy Magic Frank lived next door to me in Chicago with his two older brothers, Woody and Jerry, and their mother. I spent quite a bit of time at their house from the age of ten until I was seventeen, and there were few dull moments. The brothers were constantly hammering on one another and their mother regularly pounded on them. All three boys were bruisers. Mealtime at their house was like a scene out of the movie *One Million B.C.*, in which the cavemen wrestled each other and tore each other's lungs out just to snatch a piece of meat.

The biggest and toughest of the three was the eldest, Jerry, also known as Moose. Moose was a legendary Chicago athlete who had starred in basketball and football in high school and then went on to play tackle and guard at two or three different universities. After the boys' father died, Moose came home and took over the family automobile insurance business, which was failing. Moose decided to specialize in insuring so-called uninsurable motorists, drivers who had been in multiple accidents or had acquired so many moving-violation citations that the more regular companies felt they were too poor a risk. The rates Moose charged these people were exorbitant but if they failed to pay on time Moose attached their property, usually their car, until they came across. If their collateral was insufficient, there would be other, less benign consequences.

Moose's first partner in this enterprise was a six-foot-tall, three-hundred-pound monster named Cueball Bluestein. Moose was six-three and two-twenty, so they comprised quite a tag team. Cueball was the designated enforcer, although Moose was no slouch if push came to shove came to pull some deadbeat's ear off and mail it to his wife and kids. The boys at Mid-Nite Insurance knew how to do business in Chicago.

Cueball really was a beast, though. Whenever he saw me or Frankie he'd hit us so hard on the arm or shoulder we'd carry the bruises for three weeks. The worst thing was to get caught in a narrow hallway with him where he'd ram his bulk into you against a wall, squeezing out all of your breath, then leave you gasping on the floor while he waddled away laughing. I hated him, and so did Frank.

After I left the neighborhood I kept in touch with Frankie, and through him I heard news of his brothers but I didn't know much about what had become of Cueball Bluestein, other than that at some point he'd been confined to Clark County, Nevada—which includes Las Vegas—as part of some kind of Mafia deal. I knew Cueball was a big gambler and that he'd become a hit man for the Chicago mob, but I didn't know any of the details until I had dinner with Frank one night in Chicago years later.

According to Frank, after Cueball and Moose parted company in the insurance business—though they remained friends—Cueball went to work for Dodo Saltimbocca, the Chicago crime boss. The night before Saltimbocca was scheduled to testify in front of a commission investigating organized crime, Cueball, who was as close to Saltimbocca as you could get, being his aide and confidant, shot and killed him. The other Chicago bosses thought that Saltimbocca was going to rat on them so they got Cueball to pull the trigger. For this good deed Cueball was sent to Vegas and installed as the number two man under Sammy Eufemia, for whom he labored a number of years. The Chicago mob ruled Vegas and the New York mob ruled Atlantic City and all was, if not entirely copacetic, understood.

The Chicago cops, as well as the Feds, knew that Cueball had murdered Saltimbocca, but the deal was that they wouldn't touch him as long as he remained in Clark County. All went swimmingly until Sammy Eufemia wound up piled on top of his brother, Bitsy, in a shallow grave in an Indiana cornfield. Both Bitsy and Sammy had been shot in the exact same spot in the back of their heads. Dodo Saltimbocca had been similarly executed.

Had Cueball made the move in order to become number one in Vegas? Or was it a play on the part of the New York crowd looking to horn in on forbidden territory? Frankie didn't know, he told me, and didn't want to. He did know that Cueball was currently in prison in Nevada on a ten-year rap for receiving stolen property, mostly jewelry. On his income tax form each year, Frank said, Cueball always listed his profession as "jeweler."

"He was never a nice guy," I said to Frank.

"True," Frankie said, "but he was from the neighborhood, same as us. Also same as us," said Frank, "his father died when he was young. I'm sure that's one of the reasons I got into as many fights as I did when I was a kid. I was upset."

"Maybe," I said, "but you didn't become a killer, and neither did I."

"Well," said Frank, "probably Cueball was more pissed off about it than we were."

The Brothers

I had always wanted a brother, and when my dad's second wife, Eva, had a boy, I was overjoyed. The problem was that we didn't live together and I didn't often get to see him.

Soon after my brother Willie was born, I wrote my first story. It was seven pages long, hand-printed on yellow legal paper, and titled "All in Vain." It was about two brothers who don't know they're brothers. They fight on opposite sides of the Civil War and the Confederate brother kills the Yankee brother. After the war is over the Rebel brother discovers what he's done, gets drunk in a bar, and dies in a gunfight.

Years later I was looking through my old desk at my mother's house for the story but I couldn't find it. I asked my mother what happened to it and she said she'd cleaned out the desk after I'd left home and thrown out everything that wasn't important.

Our dad died when Willie was six and I was twelve. After that I did not see my brother for ten years. When we finally did meet again we got along very well, and we continue to see each other regularly and to correspond. We don't, however, look at all alike. I'm medium tall and medium build with blue eyes and thick curly black hair, and my brother is very tall and thin with dark brown eyes and thin straight brown hair. Of the two, it's I who most closely resembles our father.

When we're together nobody ever guesses that we're brothers. Whomever we tell invariably says how strange it is that we're so different looking. "We're half brothers," my brother or I say. "We had the same father."

I've always been sorry that Dad died without ever having been together with both Willie and me at the same time. As adults, I mean, or even as adolescents. It would have made us seem more like real bothers.

Exile

One night in the early winter of 1965, when I was living in London, I accompanied my friend the Duke of Earls Court to a Middle Eastern restaurant. We were led downstairs into a dimly lit room and invited to sit on fluffy, large pillows that were carefully arranged on the floor around a small, circular wooden table. Each of us was given a hookah and a bar of Lebanese tobacco, then instructed in the use of the hookahs and told that the smoking of hashish was not allowed.

The slab of tobacco was approximately the size of a bar of hotel soap. It glowed gold and red as I carefully inhaled and exhaled, establishing a comfortable rhythm with the water pipe. As my eyes grew accustomed to the dimness I saw that other people were distributed about the room on their own pillows, smoking and talking. The room was very large and glowed gold and red like the Lebanese tobacco.

The man who had led us in came back after a while and sat down next to me. He smiled and asked how we liked the tobacco and whether the pipes were drawing properly. He was very agreeable and told us how much he enjoyed living in London. He had been there twelve years now and he liked the people very much more than the weather. He entertained all sorts of people, he said, the most famous names in England. He started his own hookah and smoked with us for several minutes before excusing himself.

It had been raining hard when we'd come in and it was still raining when we walked out again into Fulham Road. The Duke hailed a taxi and once inside instructed the driver where to take us.

"Who is that man?" I asked.

"Don't you know?" said the Duke. "He's the chap that assassinated the king of Saudi Arabia in 1953."

The downpour increased in intensity and the cabbie began to swear. It occured to me that in three weeks it would be Christmas. Today was the seventh anniversary of my father's death.

"Nice fellow, isn't he?"

"What?" I said.

"The chap there," said the Duke. "Nice fellow."

"Oh, yes," I agreed. He certainly had been very polite.

"Awfully damn nice," the Duke said, staring at the ribbons of water cascading down the window glass.

"Have you ever known anyone else who's committed a murder?" he asked.

"I'm not sure," I said.

"Well," said the Duke, "I daresay he must have had a handsome reason."

A Long Day's Night
in the Naked City

My dad had a friend in New York named Edgar Volpe whom I used to visit every so often when I was in town. He died about ten years ago but until then Edgar hung out at the Villa Luna restaurant on Grand Street between Mott and Elizabeth in Little Italy. I could usually find him there in a booth at the back talking to a couple of guys who looked like they were in a hurry. Edgar was a fat man, he weighed about two hundred and fifty pounds and stood maybe five foot eight with his shoes on. He always looked like he had plenty of time to talk.

From what little Edgar told me about his relationship with my dad I gathered that they had collaborated on a few liquor heists during the thirties. Edgar never really opened up to me and there was no reason that he should have. He was always very nice and insisted on buying me lunch at the Villa. One afternoon when I was eating linguini with clam sauce and discussing with Edgar the vicissitudes of the New York Rangers, of whom he was an avid follower, a short, wiry guy came in and over to our table and held out to

Edgar an envelope. "It's there," he said. "I'm fuckin' t'rough wid it."

Edgar didn't touch the envelope, motioning with a nod for the man to lay it on the table, which he did. "Siddown, why doncha," said Edgar. "Have some linguini." "Nah, t'anks," said the man. "I got my cab outside. I'm workin'." He shifted from foot to foot and looked quickly around the restaurant. The man was about thirty-five to forty, five-nine or -ten. He was wearing sunglasses so I couldn't see his eyes. "So we're t'rough now, right?" he said to Edgar. "Dis makes it." Edgar nodded slowly and gave the man a small half-smile. "If you say so," said Edgar. "I'm always around if you want." The wiry man gave a loud, short laugh. "I hope to fuck I won't," he said. He looked around again and back at Edgar, then at me, then back at Edgar. "So I'm goin'," he said. "And t'anks, Mr. Volpe. T'anks a million." "Anytime," said Edgar.

The man left and Edgar slowly picked up the envelope and put it into his inside jacket pocket. "Funny guy," Edgar said to me. "He was a cop. Then he's moonlightin' one night guardin' some buildin's over onna West Side an' almost gets his eye shot out. Some fancy-lookin' white broad is out stoppin' cars—Mercedes, Cadillacs, Jags, expensive models—an' tellin' the driver she got a flat tire or somethin'. Then as the driver's about to give her a lift, a black guy dressed like a bum comes up behind the broad and drags her into an alley. Naturally, the driver jumps out and chases the attacker. I mean this broad is a doll, dressed to the nines, a real fox, an' the guy thinks he's got somethin', see, so he goes to help her, right? The black guy takes off when he sees the driver comin' and drops the broad. The driver comforts the broad, takes her into his car. Asks her where she wants to go. She puts a gun to his head, opens the door, and the black guy gets in the back, also wid a gun. They're workin' together, right? They rob the driver and have him drive to his house or apartment, which they clean out the jewels and cash. Nice scam. Worked thirty-two times inna row until my pal there, the cop who's moonlightin' in order to save money for his weddin',' spots this couple in the act.

"Sonny there, the cop, tries to pull the black guy outta this Mercedes, an' the broad shoots him inna head. Sonny's lyin' onna ground next to the car and the black guy falls out right onna Sonny. Sonny's bleedin' like crazy but figures if he's gonna die he's not goin' down alone, so he plugs the nigger, passes out.

"When he wakes up, Sonny's inna hospital wid his eye bandaged. He's alive an' the doctors tell 'im a couple operations an' maybe he won' hafta lose his right eye. The nigger's dead; the broad got away clean. While he's inna hospital, the broad Sonny's engaged to never even comes to see him. She thinks he's gonna die anyway, right? He'd already given her, what, maybe ten, fourteen t'ousand dollars for the wedding. She's why he's fuckin' moonlightin' inna first place. So while he's inna hospital fightin' for his life she runs off wid some other guy. By the time Sonny gets out he's in deep shit 'cause the police department insurance policy won't cover him since he was off duty an' workin' for somebody else. So he needs money, he comes to me. He's suin' the insurance company, the owner of the buildin' he's guardin' that night, the cops, everybody he can think of. On top of that he's afraid to go see the broad t'rew him over 'cause he'd put six inna her. Now he's pushin' a hack tryna get back on his feet. I give him a good deal, plenya time to pay me back, right? Why not. Your dad, he helped out plenya guys."

Listening to Willie

I went to see my dad's old friend, Willie "the Hero" Nero, who was now living in retirement in Las Vegas. A very old man, Willie nevertheless spoke with enthusiasm about the old days. I found that if I interrupted him, asked questions, it broke his train of thought and disturbed him. He knew why I was there and was willing to talk. All I had to do was listen.

"Your dad was a straight guy," Willie said. "I could always trust him to do whatever it was he said he'd do. No complaints on that score. Too bad he died so young, the future was his.

"Your dad never done nothin' really illegal that I know of, except maybe buying hot cases of booze now and again, or a ring maybe. The games never bothered nobody, the gambling, I mean. Look at all this, anyway, Vegas. A book is a book, you know? You got to pay off when you got to, otherwise it's yours. Everybody played back then. The cops knew it and let it be. Better than dope, you know? And the whores was somebody else's bailiwick.

"Rudy held on to things for people, he was good at keeping things in a safe place. People could trust him, plus he was a tough customer, he didn't take no shit never and he wouldn't rat. Two important points. Rare qualities for *any* business. *Any* business.

"I was always a soft guy myself. I wasn't much with a gun in my hand. I held one if I had to but what's the point? The real rough stuff was left to crazies, meshuggeners such as Dago La Gamba and Dolf Valentino—'Kid Valentines' he called himself because he'd leave a valentine as a callin' card on the body. A psycho with a sense of humor.

"You know I was from the West Coast originally. Portland, where my old man ran a livery business. A taxi service with horses. I knew all about horses when I was a kid. Our name was Varchov, from Poland, Polish Jews. My parents couldn't wait to get out of there, the Polack anti-Semites. I was short—I still am—and pushy, so I got the name Nero, after the emperor, right? Even before I left Portland that was, before I went to L.A. From L.A. I went to Chicago.

"Your dad was a kid when I met him. A bright kid, he went to college. You know that, I'm sure. That was rare, strange. He had an education but talked like he never been off Maxwell Street, Taylor Street. But you couldn't fool him, he was that way.

"One time we did something together. It was when your dad was startin' out. He came with me to Hollywood. I was sent because of my familiarity with the place. I'd lived there, as I told you, after Portland. We had some business with

Zingermann, the old man, the father who produced all the big movies. He had a young wife who'd gotten in dutch and B.Z. Zingermann asked the boys in Chicago to help out. We did, then Rudy, your dad, and I, delivered her out to the old man. Look at me talkin' about an old man, now I'm older'n Zingermann was then.

"Anyway, we go out to L.A. and drop off the doll and B.Z. says stick around, learn the movie business. Have a holiday. So Rudy and I hang out for a few days, we gamble, at first it feels good in the sun with no overcoat, you know. One day we're on the lot and they're in the middle of makin' *Road to Fairyland*, with Little Ida MacFarland. She was a big child star who later killed herself as you probably heard. Cut her own throat one night, an unhappy kid. She was maybe nine years old when your dad and I were out there. So between scenes we go over to her trailer near the set there to see the old man. A flunky opens the door and there's B.Z. himself—'The Big Gun of Filmdom' they used to call him— stretched out on the couch with his pants down around his ankles while Little Ida performed as convincing an act of fellatio as you ever could hope to see.

"B.Z. never saw us, I don't think. He had his eyes closed and we backed off quick as we could. Ida saw us, though. She didn't miss a stroke, just raised one eyebrow the way she did all the time in the movies and stared straight at us for one solid moment before the flunky closed the door. B.Z. must have been in his seventies then.

"There never was anything nice about that Hollywood business. Your dad and I had a good laugh lots of times about that Ida MacFarland thing. I think after that we went down to San Diego on that trip, bought a warehouse to ship gum machines from or something. I don't remember.

"Just know your dad was no crook. If he cheated anybody they deserved it. This is a different world now and I don't mind knowing I ain't got a hell of a long time left in it."

Waking after Having Fallen Asleep while Reading Rimbaud's *Les Déserts de l'amour*

I am puzzled but pleased by this dream. There was my father, dead two dozen years, in a new flannel shirt and gray trousers, sitting in the kitchen talking to me. There was activity in the kitchen but I couldn't tell who else was there, they were blanketed in swirling gray; women, perhaps, in maid's uniforms, rather old and bustling about, as oblivious to us as my father seemed to them.

My father spoke softly to me, serenely, as if he had been away and was soon to leave again, allowing us only this small conversation in an unrecognizable kitchen. He was much as I'd known him the several years I had, and a child was what I appeared in the dream, though I'd never remembered him so plainly dressed; and his speech fell inaudible beneath the noise of the kitchen. I did not mind the noise and stared straight at him, his body centered, seated at the table, but spinning successively left to right, too, in a semicircle above me, drawing my attention away from the words on his lips I was straining to hear. I did not, however, want to push the moment; I felt satisfied with the time we had.

My father suddenly disappeared, leaving me alone at the table. The kitchen was silent, black pans floating in frosty gray. My age was now indeterminate. The dream turned over, revealing a prison visiting room, again gray and guarded by the others present, only more obviously so because of their badges and guns, guards of the prison.

Again I was seated, talking to my mother's fourth husband through the mesh sheeting, though he could be plainly seen. He was happy, he told me, it was not that bad at all; he wasn't bothered by the need to please my mother, to make a living. The men inside were amiable enough, or did not talk; at least they left him alone. His cell was livable, he said, and he did not mind the food. He had time to think and joke with the others. He was staying in, he said, until he understood why he was there.

The dream faded, and I was awakened by the crying of my baby daughter, as if her tears, elongated gray and silver, were rolling limp like mercury down the back of my neck.

Riffraff

In the summer of 1984 I traveled to Chicago to see Louella Franklin, an old girlfriend of Dago La Gamba—an adversary of my father's—and a former showgirl at the Club Alabam. She was living in the Whitehall, a well-to-do residence hotel on the Near North Side around the corner from the Seneca, the hotel I'd lived in with my mother and father until I was five years old.

Louella was a well-preserved seventy. She wore an auburn wig, her eyes were heavily made up, she wore red fingernail polish and plenty of jewelry. She smoked constantly—long, thin filter-tipped cigarettes—and sipped at a water glass filled with Johnnie Walker Black Label. The voice was a surprise—rather than the throaty huskiness I expected, Louella spoke in a lilting, singsong, exceedingly pleasant high register. When she smiled, which was often, she revealed even, sparkling-white capped teeth.

"Riffraff," she said. "That's all any of them were. Oh, your dad was okay, he could be swell. Albert, too—he was a Good Joe. But Dago, a bum. Also that Strazza and Biaggi. Real scum. It was Willie Nero's boys knocked off Dago, you see. I'm certain of it. What he knew would have put any of them away, and times were changing, a new regime, you see.

"After I came to Chicago from New York, Dago and I went together for years, maybe ten. His wife knew about me, but she was smart, kept her mouth shut and took whatever she wanted. I never wanted to get married. What did I need that for? I was ahead of my time. Dago took care of me good most of the time, and when he was inside I had other friends. Dago didn't mind what he didn't know—what he didn't *want* to know, you see?

"Listen, all these guys were up to no good. That was their *business*! At least what the cops said was no good. It was no good only if they couldn't control it. You see? Dago was the one who took care of the problems, ever since Capone. He had the tavern—the Bomb Shelter—and they had food there, good food. That was his front, like Rudy had the liquor store. Some of them were in the trucking business, or warehouses, or had a couple stalls down on South Water Market. Everybody had a face to show.

"Rudy and Dago had a falling out, that's true. It wasn't too long after the Beau Jack–Jake La Motta fight that Christmas. [Miss Franklin's memory is incorrect. Beau Jack, a lightweight, and Jake La Motta, a middleweight, never fought on that or any other Christmas.] Between Christmas and New Year's it must have been. Dago and Rudy went to the fight together, at the stadium, I think. The La Motta fight must have been before Christmas, I forget the year. Forty years ago! I was still a kid then. The argument had to do with a bet on the fights. I know La Motta won, by decision, so I guess it was supposed to have been a knockout. I don't remember who was supposed to knock out who, but because there wasn't a knockout there was something queer about the payoff.

"After that Christmas Rudy didn't come over to the Shelter and Dago didn't buy his liquor from Rudy anymore. It was too bad because I liked your dad. He was a generous guy, if he liked you. If he didn't, well—none of these characters really trusted anyone until after they'd done business with them. It was a tough world they made and you couldn't fake your way through it.

"I recall that Biaggi and Strazza and maybe Albert were involved in some kind of fencing operation. Maybe Dago, too. It was very clean except that Biaggi was always getting into too many things at once; that's what I heard, anyway. Spreading himself too thin. There probably was a case involving stolen bonds, I don't know. Nobody told me anything so specific, and I didn't want to know. What I didn't know couldn't hurt me, you see?

"They found Dago in the trunk of a car after he'd been missing for a couple of days. He'd been shot on Taylor Street and kidnapped. Nero had it in for him. Dago's wife and mother carried on something terrible. He had a mother like in a Jimmy Cagney movie, you know? 'He was a good boy, he always took care of me.' That kind of thing.

"Rudy ran around plenty in the old days, before your mother, during, and after. For a long time it was with that blond, Diane. She worked in the liquor store once in a while. Later I guess she took up with his pal Albert. He was a sweet guy, actually, Albert. He had a thick accent; he was Cajun, a real one. His family, parents, brothers, sisters, still lived in shacks in the swamps down in Louisiana when I knew him. I don't know how he got into the rackets, but he handled a lot of business in New Orleans. He and Rudy were good pals. I think I heard Albert died about ten years ago.

"The one I admired most was Ginny Hill, Ben Siegel's girlfriend. When she told the government to go to hell. They never got a dime's worth of satisfaction out of her. She ended up in Switzerland, I guess it was, married to a ski instructor, before she died. She was a beauty, too, in her day, from Alabama. I always respected her attitude; what she knew was nobody's business but hers. That's the way I feel, too. I never said a good or bad word I didn't want to."

Renoir's *Chemin montant dans les hautes herbes*

The path on the hillside is a stripe of light, a three-dimensional effect. There is nothing theoretical about this: everything is where it is supposed to be. Not merely light and shadow and balance and color but the *unprepared for*, the element that informs as well as verifies the work. As the light in the Salle Caillebotte in the Jeu de Paume changes the painting changes, too—like the sun slowly emerging from behind a cloud, it opens and displays more of itself.

The people and the setting are from a previous century: women and children descending the path. There is absolutely nothing savage about the picture. Flowers, fruit trees, foot-worn path, wooden fence—nothing to disturb. The element of feeling is calm; difficulty disappears.

An early summer afternoon in the house in Chicago. I'm ten years old. The sky is very dark. A thunderstorm. I'm sitting on the floor in my room, the cool tiles. The rain comes, at first very hard, then soft. I'm playing a game by myself. Nobody else is around, except, perhaps, my mother, in another part of the house. There is and will be for a while nothing to disturb me. This is my most beloved childhood memory, an absolutely inviolable moment, totally devoid of difficulty. It's the same feeling I have when I look at Renoir's *Chemin montant dans les hautes herbes.* I doubt very seriously if my father would have understood this feeling.

My
Mother's
Story

~

The summer that I was sixteen I worked as an assistant to the director of the San Carlos Opera Company. The director was a friend of my mother's; he would dictate to me in a heavy Italian accent, always with a blue beret on his head. He never dictated without that beret on. I'd have to make his imperfect sentences into understandable English. It was fun for me, I made some money and got to meet many of the great opera stars of the day. One of them, whose name I've now forgotten, noticed me staring at him in awe and said, very gently, "Do close your mouth, young lady." That job and modeling were the only two types of work I had until many years later.

My high school boyfriend, Hal, went into the navy following graduation; he was stationed on the lakefront in Chicago. Every Sunday night we'd meet and have dinner at Rickett's, which was right around the corner from the pharmacy where I'd gone to have my eyedrop and ointment prescriptions filled. Once in a while Hal and I would drop into the drugstore and I'd say hello to Rudy, the pharmacist who'd been so nice to me. Rudy was about twenty years older than I was, a stocky, powerfully built man of average height. Rudy was not very good-looking but, as I say, he was extremely nice and helped me out.

One evening I was standing on the corner of Chicago and Rush waiting for Hal when I heard a car horn tooting and tooting. I turned around and saw a Cadillac at the curb, filled with sailors. At the wheel was Rudy, the pharmacist. I didn't recognize him at first and turned away, paying them no attention. Rudy got out of the car and came up to me and started a conversation. As soon as I saw that it was Rudy I got very friendly and he asked me if I'd like to come along with him and the boys and have something to eat. I told him that I was waiting for my date and just then Hal came up. "Oh, is this your date?" Rudy said, and Hal said hello to him. It turned out that they knew each other, or at least Hal knew who Rudy was; as I was to find out very shortly, everybody who had any business in that part of town knew Rudy, from the high to the low. Rudy Winston was a popular figure in the club district.

"Well," said Rudy, "can I treat you kids to something? Do you want to come along? I'm just giving these sailors a lift out to the Great Lakes Naval base." We told him no, that we had a time limit because Hal had to be back on duty soon, and that was the end of it. The next day I got a phone call from Rudy. He'd gone through every McCloud in the book until he found the right one. He asked me to have dinner with him, and was extremely polite about it. I told him that I was going to have dinner nearby with my folks that evening and promised that I would come into the store and say hello. My mother and father and I did go in, and he gave them a tour of the place, in the back and all around. Rudy was very charming and they liked him, they were impressed.

None of us knew that in the basement was probably the biggest bookie joint in the city of Chicago! I really didn't know anything about that kind of thing in those days. I was just home from my year and a half of college.

After that I went out alone with Rudy for dinner a few times, and he took me around a little bit. We went to the racetrack and I started smoking. I felt like I was growing up, but I was very proper and Rudy acted like a gentleman at all times. He gave me gold cigarette holders and gold cases, which I promptly lost or gave away. I had no sense of the value of things. And Rudy didn't care, he'd just laugh. He seemed to have an endless supply of money, always paying for things with cash, large bills; but he wasn't ostentatious, he had good manners and knew how to have a good time. He was a big drinker but never got drunk. Actually, he was an amazing character and I was fascinated by him. He proposed marriage to me but I was not at all interested; I was just a young girl and wanted to get around, to see the world. I told him, "I haven't seen anything of life yet," and Rudy said, "I'll show you anything you like." He was terrific to know but marriage wasn't what I wanted.

I was going out with several guys then, one of whom was a law student at Northwestern. We'd ride bicycles in Evanston, around the university, and buy ice cream out in No Man's Land along the North shore. He was a nice boy who later became a well-known attorney in Chicago. So I had young friends, too, but I was intrigued by Rudy Winston.

I wondered where he got all that money; and I did like the high life, which he knew so well. Whenever I went out of town, like when I returned to Texas, Rudy sent me presents and wrote me little notes; and when I came back to Chicago he was always there, waiting to pick me up at the train station. I was flattered by this kind of attention. It was hard not to be.

My father was really the one who always wanted to protect me, to see that I didn't have to deal with anything, to worry. He wanted the best for me, to just be a beautiful playgirl. I remember him saying to my mother, "Peggy's a playgirl, a pretty playgirl." And I didn't know what he meant by it. He liked Rudy Winston; he felt that Rudy would take care of me, protect me. Buck liked Rudy, too; or at least he respected him. He knew who he was, that he was involved in the rackets in some way. Rudy was a Jew, the family name had been Weinstein until Rudy's brother had changed it, and that made him seem more exotic to me. And all of the crazy characters he knew! Big guys in immaculate, hand-tailored three-piece suits with fancy handkerchiefs sticking out of the breast pocket; weaselly little men in hats who were whispering in Rudy's ear all the time, running in and out. I'd never seen anything like this before. Rudy seemed to be at his store day and night, always willing to take me somewhere, to jump in the big blue Cadillac and take a drive. He offered me a car, or the use of one, the second time we met. What kind of man was this? I wondered. But my family liked him and he certainly was different than anyone I'd ever met before.

~

After I decided that I didn't want to go back to the University of Texas, where, by the way, I'd won a campus beauty contest—despite my allergies!—which resulted in my being offered a modeling contract by a large agency (I turned it down because I was really in bad shape due to the eczema), I went to New York, to Long Island, to visit my aunt Maria.

Aunt Maria had a mansion in Hewlett Bay, a big stone house filled with paintings and sculpture and all kinds of would-be actors and actresses, writers and artists, coming and going. She let them use the house as a weekend retreat, fed them, and probably gave most of them money if they needed it. Her own children used to complain about how cheap she was, how she never gave them a dime, instead throwing all of her money away on deadbeat actors and artists. But Aunt Maria did what she wanted; she liked being a part of the art scene, being a benefactress, and she didn't care what her kids thought. I suppose she had a little romance now and then with one of the guys she helped out; I really didn't think much about it at the time, and I don't see why it should have bothered her children the way it apparently did. My mother told me they would complain to her about how Aunt Maria spent her money and about her liaisons. So far as I was concerned, Aunt Maria was a wonderful woman: generous, kind, maybe a bit pretentious in her manner and conversation, but a good soul.

Rudy Winston telephoned me often at Aunt Maria's, and sent the usual little gifts, so we stayed in contact, but after a while I got very bored staying out in Long Island. I enjoyed listening to the people's stories, about their artistic struggles and difficulties, eating well and being taken care of by Aunt Maria and her staff, but I was feeling restless and decided to move into New York City. The war was on and everything was booming in the city. I loved the bright lights and all of the activity. I got a room in a woman's hotel in midtown Manhattan, the Conroy, I think it was called; it's gone now. I later found out that there were some very high-priced call girls working out of that hotel, but I didn't know about it at the time. I was very naive, nineteen years old, and everything fascinated me.

I looked up the modeling agency that had been interested in me after I won the beauty contest at Texas, and started getting some jobs, mostly modeling hats and jewelry. I had some money in my pocket and felt better than I had in a long time. My aunt Maria was upset, however; I was supposed to be in her care and she feared for my safety in the big city. I had been very protected up to that point and I understood her concern. She called my mother and my brother—who was now a commander in the navy and living with Laura Mae in Philadelphia—and told them I was too young to be living on my own in Manhattan. She was afraid I'd be led astray. Buck kept in touch; I went down to Philadelphia to visit him and his wife in their beautiful, large apartment near

Rittenhouse Square—they had two baby grand pianos!—
and assured them that I'd be all right, that I was working
and not to worry. My brother was busy with his military
duties and couldn't spend much time with me, and Laura
Mae was involved with her society friends, so I went back to
New York after a short time.

I dyed my hair black—my long auburn hair—and piled
it up on my head, wore some jewelry and only a very little
makeup. I succeeded in looking older than I was but retained
my legitimate, innocent look. My mother wrote that she was
ill and wanted me to come home but I was enjoying myself
too much. She was practically bedridden by this time
because of her worsening heart condition, and I knew that if
I went back I'd have to spend my time nursing her. I decided
to be a little selfish and stay in New York, telling my father
to make sure Rose had enough help around the house. He
assured me that he would take care of it; his fur business was
going well, he said, and they could afford a full-time maid,
so that lessened my guilt feelings. My mother really was
more afraid for me than she was feeling sicker; she just
wanted her little girl home.

In New York, through my modeling job, I was introduced
to many different people, and I started to get around. I had
a different date every night and was taken to the best restaurants and nightclubs. I learned how to take care of myself.
This was in 1943. Men offered to set me up in apartments, to
pay all of my bills, and that kind of thing, and I'd just laugh

and be nice to them if I felt like it. Then one night I went to a party Harry Cohn, the boss of Columbia Pictures, gave at the Sherry-Netherland Hotel, or the Warwick, one of those. I couldn't believe how many beautiful young, blond cuties he had sitting around, all starlets or would-be starlets. It was an amazing party, a great deal of fun, and it was there that I met an exiled White Russian count, Vladimir Kozeny, who became my steady boyfriend.

Kozeny—for some reason I can't recall now I always called him by his last name—had a heart condition, and in his apartment in the Ansonia Hotel on Broadway he had a push-button bed, the kind that was in three sections, because he wasn't supposed to lie down flat. He took me in hand and I thought this was wonderful. The Ansonia was full of mad composers and zany characters who looked like the Marx Brothers. I think Gustav Mahler had once lived there. Kozeny was pals with all of them, they all knew and deferred to him; he was still royalty in that place. Kozeny bought me all kinds of clothes, gorgeous things, only the best. Despite his bad heart we were always on the town—he was proud of me, his young thing, the beautiful model, and he loved showing me off.

Of course all I had to do for Kozeny was go out with him; he really didn't care for more than a little kissing and to put his hand on my leg and have me fuss over him a bit. He wasn't that old, he was in his fifties, and I liked him very much. We'd go to parties and he'd wear a coat with tails and a large red sash across his chest. I didn't realize who most of the people were that I was being introduced to and mixing with: Prince This and Princess That, movie people like Cohn and big-time mobsters. It was the latter that led to my return to Chicago. I didn't know it at the time, but one of those mob guys happened to mention my name to Rudy one day on the phone—I didn't know about Rudy's involvement with these people at this point—and I guess he told my mother or father about it. Anyway, my mother got on the phone and told me that if I didn't come home immediately there was going to be a death in the family. I didn't know if she meant mine or hers but I left New York, and when I got back to Chicago I cried and cried. My mother asked me what was wrong and I said, "I think I'm in love with Kozeny." So my mother got on the phone again and called Kozeny. She told him that if he attempted to contact her daughter he'd be exiled right out of the world. She really did! She went wild and threatened to get Rudy's palookas after him. And this was really the first I heard of Rudy's connections. Of course he was there to welcome me back; he chastised me mildly for running around like I had but Rudy was really very nice and understanding. I'd been in New York for a year or so, I'd had a wonderful fling. I was just twenty and about to begin a totally new phase of my life.

~

So I was home again. "School or work," said my mother. I didn't want to work, I hated working; modeling was all I knew and I couldn't stand having to smile and be constantly scrutinized like a piece of meat. I'd done that secretarial job for the opera the summer I was sixteen but the idea of doing that again was even worse, and I wasn't really very adept at shorthand and typing. I thought it better to get married. All of my girlfriends were married; but they'd married their high school boyfriends and they were poor, just barely getting along. I didn't want that.

Rudy Winston, of course, was still after me, and I did like him very much. He was very polite and generous and quite an interesting person in his own right. I remember the night he taught me to drive. We came out of the theater and he was suffering from the flu; he'd gotten so sick in the theater that we'd had to leave before the show was over. "Drive the car," he told me, and gave me the keys; he could barely sit up straight in the passenger seat. "I don't have a license," I told him. "I've never even had a lesson!" "Drive it!" he said. It was his new Cadillac—he always had a new Cadillac. So I drove it. We had the wildest ride either of us had ever had. I drove him home and then I drove myself home; he let me keep the car. I went around corners twenty thousand miles an hour! And Rudy didn't even bat an eye. He just said, "That's wonderful, Peggy. I thought you told me you'd never driven a car before." He was incredible; he had great faith in me. He said do this and do that, and here's first gear and here's second. I'd never met anyone like him in my life. He let me do whatever I wanted to. "If you want the car, keep it," he said; and I thought, what a strange man!

Now he began to give me more expensive and glamorous presents. I could go into any store on Michigan Avenue and charge whatever I liked to Rudy. Just sign and take a nice dress, a hat. My mother wanted the good life for me, and she liked Rudy, but he wasn't handsome enough for her. She wanted me to marry a guy like Hal French, a tall, good-looking Hal French with money, not a burly, tough guy like Rudy Winston. My father and Rudy got along great; they both liked to drink, and Rudy would take Jack out and they'd have a wonderful time with plenty of booze and show-girls. My father would say, "That Rudy's a swell fellow, you know." And my mother would say, "You don't want to marry him, Peggy. How could you be in the same bathroom with that man? I don't want my beautiful daughter in the same bathroom with a gangster."

My mother got very weird about all of this. She got along all right with Rudy, and didn't hesitate to invoke his name when she threatened poor Vladimir Kozeny on the phone, but marrying him was something else. She knew Rudy had proposed to me several times by now and that I'd developed a mind of my own. Her heart was weak, she couldn't argue as vociferously as she had in the past, and she began to use this argument, based on her health, to try to dissuade me from marrying Rudy. So I was torn between my loyalty to her and the life of luxury Rudy kept promising that I would have if I married him. I truly did not know what to do. My father remained noncommittal about the marrying part; he and Rudy were buddies but he left the decision to me.

Rudy went to my mother and said, "Look, Peggy's a nervous wreck. She wants to marry me but she doesn't want to hurt you, she wants to do what you say; she's a good girl. I never had a real mother," he told her, "my mother died before I got to know her, but I'm sure she would have loved Peggy like I do. I'll make Peggy happy, Rose. I'll give her everything she wants and take care of you, too. One thing I'd like from you and Jack, though," he said, "is a big wedding. I'll pay for it, but I want you to put it on. Peggy is the most important thing in the world to me and I want everybody to know about it. I'll be good to her, Rose. Give us your blessing."

My mother said yes, and she and my father paid for the wedding, not Rudy. There must have been five hundred people at the wedding; almost all of them were Rudy's friends and acquaintances, people I'd never seen before. Only about fifty of my friends were there, school girlfriends and their husbands who came in and turned up their noses. Most of them were straight, middle-class kids, and Rudy's crowd was a very different league. I looked stunning in an original Lola Soave dress, a long gown, and the kids from my school, my old friends whom I hadn't really seen or been in touch with for some time, didn't quite know what to make of it. I said good-bye to them at my wedding; we were in separate worlds now. Even my own relatives were jealous, surprised. They—except for Aunt Maria, who couldn't come—were just getting by, just starting to make it, and all of a sudden I was already there; it looked like the big time to them and I guess it was. It was a shock to them. The party was held at the Blackstone Hotel. The mayor was there, we received a wire from the governor wishing us well, and I remember my mother whispering to my father, "Jack, who was that nice man I was just speaking with?" "Al Capone's brother," he told her. I believe Al Capone was in Alcatraz by this time.

Rudy and I went to Lake Placid, New York, for our honeymoon. We walked in the woods and went swimming— though Rudy couldn't swim, he never did learn how. There were all kinds of things Rudy couldn't do but tried for my sake. He'd never bowled before, and I loved to bowl, so he'd just pick up a ball and, in his own unorthodox fashion, roll the ball down the alley a hundred miles an hour—he had tremendous strength—and knock all the pins down! He said he was the best dancer in the world, but he didn't know how to dance at all. We got out on the dance floor and he danced every dance. He was a riot! He did everything even if he couldn't do it. Rudy had no fear of anything, and he had a great sense of humor to go along with an outrageous temper. He never showed the temper to me but I'd heard stories about him from his friends. Rudy did some business in New York while we were there, in the city. I went shopping and he saw whomever he had to, he never discussed it with me. We went out on the town with two sons of the owner of a large theater chain; they were with their girlfriends, not their wives, and afterward Rudy told me he wouldn't run around on me like that. To tell the truth the thought hadn't crossed my mind; I was used to the behavior of my father and brother and I hadn't intended to make Rudy promise me anything. I was glad to be married but I hadn't really considered what that meant.

~

When Rudy and I came home from our honeymoon I wanted to get an apartment or a house but Rudy said no, we had to live near his store, near Rush Street, so we rented a suite in the Seneca Hotel on Chestnut Street. I knew the Castle boys, who owned the drugstore in the Palmer House, where we used to go often for dinner, and they offered me a job selling perfume; they wanted me to talk to customers about their line of fine French perfumes. This was to be a part-time job, more or less at my own convenience, but Rudy said no, I couldn't work, not his wife; he would give me an allowance of twenty-five dollars a week. I could go into any store and charge whatever I wanted; I could eat in the finest restaurants and never be presented with a bill; I could have my own Cadillac or any other car I wanted; but I wasn't allowed to have any cash in my hand other than the twenty-five dollars Rudy gave me each week. He was the boss.

It was a fast crowd that stayed at the Seneca in those days. Most of the guests lived there on a permanent basis or else kept a room for whenever they might need it. Eddie Danillo, who owned the Milwaukee Ace brewery, lived next door to us. Eddie was a nice guy. I knew he was connected with the Mafia, but I didn't think that was a big deal; everybody I met with Rudy had shady dealings. Danillo owned a couple of clothing stores, too, and one day he

knocked on our door and gave me a box with a big ribbon
on it. He said, "This is for you. I hope you like it," and then
he left. There was a very nice hat in the box, from one of his
stores. I liked the hat and wore it that night to dinner.

We were just leaving the restaurant when who should
come in but Eddie Danillo. "Gee, that hat looks great on
you," he said to me. I thanked him and said to Rudy, "Yes,
Eddie gave me this hat today. Wasn't that nice of him?"
"Eddie gave you that hat?" Rudy said. "Yes, why?" I asked.
"Wait outside for me, Peggy," Rudy told me. "I'll be right
there." I went outside and the next thing I knew there was a
loud crash from inside the restaurant. I ran back in and there
was Eddie Danillo on the floor with pieces of glass all over
him: Rudy had knocked him down through a plate-glass
window in the foyer. Rudy was calm and smiling. The maître
d' was saying to him. "It's all right, Mr. Winston, we'll take
care of everything, there's no problem, no problem." Rudy
and I left and I said, "You're crazy. Why did you knock Eddie
down? Because he gave me a hat?" Rudy stopped and looked
at me; he wasn't smiling. "I knocked him down because he
didn't *ask me* first if it was all right to give you the hat." "But
he's in the Mafia, isn't he?" I said. "You can't go around
beating up guys in the Mafia!" Rudy just laughed. "You
know," he said, "that hat really does look good on you."
The next day or maybe the day after there was an item in
one of the newspaper gossip columns about Rudy knocking
somebody through a plate-glass window, but Eddie's name

wasn't mentioned. After that Eddie and I always smiled and said hello to one another whenever we met, but he never gave me any more presents.

I became immersed in Rudy's world. Most of his so-called friends I had no use for. One of his closest buddies was a detective from the local precinct named Bill Moore. What a rotten guy he was. Every once in a while he'd use me to identify a suspect for some crime or another. Of course I'd never seen the guy before in my life. "He's no good, Peggy," Bill would say, "that's the guy who did it." And I'd have to say yes, I was there at the scene, I saw it on the street, I was passing by. Oh, it was horrible. I did it because Rudy said go on, help Bill out, he's a pal. I refused to ever testify at any trials but that didn't matter, they never asked me to do that, only to identify someone in a lineup. Who knows who they were or what they'd really done, if anything, or what happened to them?

Every now and then I'd be coming to the pharmacy when Rudy didn't expect me and there would be some policemen carting him off to jail. He'd shout, "Don't worry, Peggy, I'll be back in an hour!" And he would be. This was because of the book they were running in the basement. Rudy would have to make large "donations" to the Policemen's Benevolent Association so that he wouldn't get busted too often. "Why not?" he'd joke, "I'm a benevolent guy."

Rush Street was glorious in those days: the nightclubs were flourishing, business was good; it was a twenty-four-hour part of town. It was exciting, but I was picking up the wrong values. My mother didn't like it, didn't like the life I was leading. There was a great deal of drinking and we went out every night for dinner, which I did not want; I loved to cook, I was a good cook, my mother had taught me, and I begged Rudy to let me make him dinner at home. But then he'd show up with some stranger, some drunk, and I wouldn't let him in the house. "But this guy is a celebrity," Rudy would say. I'd get angry and slam the door on them. "I don't care who it is," I'd yell, "he's dead drunk. I don't want him in here!"

There were some nice people, though, like Barney Ross, the former boxing champion. Barney used to come into the suite at the Seneca and play the piano and tell me his life story, which was pathetic. He'd become a junkie while he was in the military hospital recovering from his war wounds. Barney was on and off the hop when I knew him; I never knew if the light was on or off, as we used to say, but he was a sweetheart. A lot of boys, of course, like Eddie Danillo, were mob guys—we never mentioned the word Mafia unless we were alone—but then there were others. Dick Bagdasarian, an Armenian who'd made a fortune as a bootlegger in the twenties, lived across the hall from us. He and his wife would go out and give their dog, a poodle, to their chauffeur and tell him to walk it. Bobby, the chauffeur, would drive the dog over to Rudy's store, put it up on the counter and have a cup of coffee. Years later my son Jimmy would sit at that counter and dunk doughnuts in the coffee and feed it to the organ-grinder's pet monkey and the Bagdasarians' poodle. Another neighbor was Buddy Harvey, who was married to one of Tommy Manville's ex-wives—the eighth, I think—and I loved her. Sunny Ainsworth was her name, she was okay in my book.

One time my mother came to visit and she went to the hairdresser in the building. I came walking in and the hairdresser or the manicurist said, "Look at that young punk, with that ten-thousand-dollar mink coat. Who does she think she is anyway?" And my mother said, "That's my daughter." My folks would come and have Sunday dinner with us, but my mother was becoming increasingly disturbed by my life, and so was I.

Then I got pregnant. I remember wearing my little pea jacket and blue beret and going to the gynecologist with my mother; Dr. Marshall, who was the finest gynecologist in Chicago, a wonderful man, who's gone now. Dr. Marshall confirmed it and I was thrilled that I was going to have a child, my mother was heartbroken. "You're too young," she told me, "No, I'm not," I said. "I've been married over a year. This is great. I want a nice little girl to keep me company. I'm alone so often at night."

I really wanted my own house or apartment, I disliked living in a hotel. I knew Rudy liked it, but I wanted a place that I could furnish myself, to have my own things, my own furniture. I wanted to be able to clean my own house, not have a hotel maid. Rudy loved the fast life, living it up; he'd consume at least a bottle of sparkling burgundy or champagne with dinner every night, even on those rare occasions he'd allow me to cook a meal for him alone. There was so much heavy drinking around me! Rudy could drink two bottles of wine with dinner and then go on drinking Irish whiskey all night, until four or five in the morning and he'd never be drunk. Other people would fall out, collapse, but not Rudy. He was a prodigious drinker and the amazing thing was that he always kept his wits; he never lost control of the situation.

We lived on the sixteenth floor and one night while I was lying in bed, thinking about my life, a bird flew in the open window. I was really petrified by this bird that was madly careening around the room, going around and around. This was after I was pregnant, I already had a big stomach. I called down to the desk and asked them for help, to get the bird out. They thought I was out of my mind, or that I'd been drinking. I said no, there's a bird going wild in here and I'm not drinking or anything. The bird was batting itself against the walls and splattering blood all over the place. And I thought, this is a bad sign; I'd never been superstitious before, but I couldn't help having this thought. This is no good, I thought, what does it mean? Finally a bellhop came up and knocked on the door. He came in and looked at me; the bird had stopped knocking into walls and was cowering on the floor in a corner. I showed the bellboy where it was and then he knew I wasn't crazy, and he took it out.

The bird was the first "sign" I had that I recognized. Many years later, the night after my mother's funeral, I was sitting in my bedroom in the house on Rockwell Street with my son Jimmy when a giant golden moth appeared at the window and began banging itself against the glass. It was the middle of winter and there were no moths that I knew of, especially large golden ones like that, flying around outside at that time of year. My first thought was that it was the spirit of my mother, it was Rose coming back to see me. The moth frightened me even more than the bird had, and I remember turning off the light and waiting in the dark, hugging Jimmy, for a half hour or so. When I turned the light on again the moth was gone, but I couldn't shake the conviction that it had been a manifestation of my mother.

Rudy's older brother Bruno was an auctioneer who also owned a couple of automobile agencies and a piece of the Chez Paree nightclub. Bruno sort of ruled Rudy, he was a tough guy, too, and Rudy looked up to him; he listened to what Bruno told him. Bruno and I got along well enough; he was much older than I was, in his forties, and we never really had too much to do with one another. Rudy and Bruno and I were at a ringside table at the Chez Paree watching Sophie Tucker when I went into labor. I almost had my baby right there on the table in the Chez Paree, but Rudy rushed me out and around to Passavant Hospital, where I had my son Jimmy—James Barry Winston, named after a brother of my father's who had died young. So I had a little boy now, not the girl I'd been certain I was going to have, and I was very happy.

Rudy was overjoyed to have a son, the first boy in the family to be born in America. Rudy had come with his family to Chicago from Austria when he was seven years old, and Bruno had yet to have children. It was a great moment for Rudy, he was so proud. Jimmy's birth was the lead item in the *Tribune* gossip column the next morning, "Talk of the Town." My hospital room was filled with flowers, all from "the boys." They overflowed into the hall and I told the nurses to please give them to the other patients who might like to have them. Everything was fine, but I couldn't get the thought of the bird out of my mind. I knew it had been a sign, but I wasn't sure of what.

~

Buck seemed to be very proud of his wife when he married her. Laura Mae Allen had university degrees both in French and mathematics and had taught both on the college level. Not only was she very bright but also glamorous; she had a marvelous figure, platinum blond hair that was completely natural and a sharp tongue. She was also extremely avaricious, acquisitive, and narrow-minded; she was anti-Semitic, anti-Catholic, and anti–people of any other color other than white. She came from a staunch Republican family that was part Scotch-English and part French. To the Allen family, there was no religion other than Episcopalian.

When I spent the summer with her and Buck in South Carolina, she instructed me that I was not to speak with any man other than an officer. When I'd come upon a nice young boy who wanted to take me out, who was not an officer, Laura Mae would say, "Don't talk to him, Peggy, he's beneath us." She presided over the dinner table like the great lady she thought she was but was not. Laura Mae thought it was just horrible that I had gone to Catholic school. I'm not sure how she dealt with the fact that Buck had been raised in a Catholic household; she certainly didn't get along very well with my parents.

However, Laura Mae took a great liking to me, and despite all of her horrible traits I managed to get along with her. She took me under her wing and sought to instruct me in what she thought was the proper manner to behave, what to like and not to like, whom to associate with, and so on.

One time Buck and I were preparing to go sailing and Laura Mae came down to the dock and said, "You can go sailing for a couple of hours, but don't forget that we have guests arriving at five o'clock. Make sure you're back in time to be dressed for dinner." Well, Buck and I didn't get back until after midnight. We sailed off in Buck's little ketch, wearing only our bathing suits, on what was at that point a nice warm day. A storm sprang up while we were out on the ocean and we lost control of the boat. I was scared to death as all of these mountainous waves came over us, almost swamping the boat. Buck kept shouting, "Bail, Peggy, bail!" I found a tin can and did what I could. In the middle of the worst part of it I suddenly found that I wasn't scared anymore. I laughed and yelled "Davy Jones's locker here we come!" Buck thought I was crazy.

We went through some rigorous maneuvers out there and finally drifted to an island; but we couldn't get off the boat because the shale was so sharp that it would cut our feet. Somehow Buck rerigged the sail and we managed to get home. Laura Mae was furious, of course, but then she saw how shaken both Buck and I were and was good to me, and helped me to bed. I had nightmares every night for a week after that, thinking that the bed was moving. I woke up screaming more than once; the window curtains were flying into the room with the breeze and I imagined they were big waves coming at me, or a big shark. It was horrible.

When I married Rudy, Laura Mae refused to attend the wedding. She made some excuse about having to stay in Philadelphia but I knew that she looked down her nose at Rudy and his people. My mother thought it no great loss that Laura Mae wasn't there; at least Buck was, and after that Laura Mae and I weren't so close. She had started drinking heavily by this time, anyway, and was already something of an alcoholic. I knew that my mother was disappointed in both Buck's and my marriages, but there really was nothing to do about it; I did feel guilty about not being able to please her. I soon learned that it was going to be even more difficult for me to be able to please myself.

~

Six months after Jimmy was born Rudy and I took a trip to the West Coast, stopping in Las Vegas on the way. We left Jimmy with his nursemaid, Flo, at my parents' house, and flew out to Vegas. Rudy had some business there. He was pals with Ben Siegel, known in the press as "Bugsy"—he *hated* that nickname and I never heard anyone call him that to his face—and Ben had told us to stay in his suite at the Flamingo.

Ben, originally from New York, where he'd been a cohort of Meyer Lansky's, had established Las Vegas as a gambling mecca for the Chicago mob. He came into Rudy's store whenever he was in town, and sent me the largest bouquet of flowers I received when Jimmy was born.

We had a great time in Vegas—Ben wasn't in town, he was in Los Angeles—and Rudy did whatever business he had to while I gambled a little and stayed by the pool. Las Vegas was still in its infancy then, and everything was very new and exciting and seemingly innocent. All of the Chicago boys were there, so it was like old home week only we were at an oasis in the desert. Everything was first class, Rudy and I were treated with the utmost deference, and I felt wonderful being on the go again.

We spent a couple of weeks in Las Vegas and then drove a rented car to Los Angeles. When we got there we checked into the old Ambassador Hotel and Rudy called Eddie Hill,

Ben's girlfriend Virginia's brother, to say hello. Ginny Hill didn't like Vegas, and spent most of her time in L.A. and Paris. I had met her several times in Chicago, where we'd gone shopping together on Michigan Avenue. Like Laura Mae, Ginny felt protective of me and liked to have me along. I was young and innocent and I suppose these older, more sophisticated women enjoyed showing me the ropes. Anyhow, as it turned out, while we had been traveling to Los Angeles from Las Vegas, Ben Siegel had been shot dead in Virginia Hill's house.

Ginny was in Europe, and Eddie said to lie low; nobody knew what might happen next. Rudy told me not to worry, that everything was all right, but I got very scared all of a sudden. I began to appreciate the reality of the situation, to really consider for the first time just who it was I had been hanging around with and what my husband did for a living. Until this point I'd been on a kind of cloud, just going along thinking that soon I'd have my little house, a nice family of my own, a husband who came home for dinner every night—a normal life. Now I saw what was going on, and I didn't want it.

Fortunately Rudy was out of the hotel room when Eddie Hill called back. "Hi, Peg," he said. "You know things are in a bit of an upheaval right now, and Virginia's out of town, but is there anything I can do for you? Can I get you a car? Take you someplace?" I just said, "Thank you so much, Ed. If we want anything we'll let you know. We have everything we need, thank you." And I never told Rudy about Eddie Hill's call; in fact, I told him that Ed had never called. I didn't want anything to do with that bunch anymore.

We stayed in L.A. for a few days. We went sightseeing and did the usual touristy things. Rudy steered clear of "business" and we had a lovely time. My father's old friend Don Gilbert, an associate from his days in the millinery business, was living there and Rudy and I looked him up. Don had married a much younger woman, also named Peggy, and we got along wonderfully. Of course they knew their way around so we put them in the backseat of our Caddy convertible and away we went, touring along the coast of California. We really had a delightful time with the Gilberts. We drove up to San Francisco and then to Reno, where Rudy received a message telling him to return to Las Vegas, which we did. Back in Vegas Rudy went off with the guys while I hung out at the pool, like before; but this time the heat began to get to me, I was uncomfortable, and I was nervous about this mob business. If they'd killed Ben Siegel they could certainly kill Rudy or anybody else. I tried to talk to Rudy about it but he said everything was fine, nothing more was going to happen, that's the way it went sometimes. Apparently Ben had overreached himself in Vegas in some way and hadn't been able to work it out. The only mention I heard made of Ben's murder was one night at dinner in Vegas when a man I'd never met before, someone in the warehouse business from Cleveland, I think, said, "It's Lansky, they wouldn't have done it without him." Rudy seemed to be in good spirits again, and that was the end of it.

I met Larry Adler, the harmonica player, in Vegas, and we became very friendly. He was a smart young man, a sweet, lovely guy; a very slight fellow, he looked as if a small breeze could blow him over. We'd sit around talking, I don't know what about. I don't even know if I had anything to say in those days. I was the playgirl, like my father had said, I looked nice all the time. It wasn't too long after this—during the McCarthy era—that poor Larry Adler was forced to leave the country, accused of being a Communist. I don't know anything about that, but he was a gentleman, a fine person, as well as a marvelous musician.

I also met some divorce lawyers from Chicago in Las Vegas. One of them was treating his girlfriend of the moment so horribly that I said to her, "How can you stand him?" I didn't know then that later on this man would represent me in my divorce from Rudy.

~

When we returned to Chicago I found that my mother's health had deteriorated. It was decided that she should spend the winter months in a warm climate so Rudy told me to take Rose and Jimmy down to Florida, where I rented a house in Miami Beach. We wound up taking a long-term lease on the house, and kept it for several years. I loved Miami; the sunshine was good for my skin and I didn't have many outbreaks of eczema. Jimmy ran around with nothing but his shorts or swimming trunks on and my mother was able to rest and sit in the sun.

Rudy would come down for weekends and we'd usually take off for Cuba. I was, naturally, never one to be alone without a gentleman around. Not that I was doing anything wrong, but when I was alone I always had a dinner date and so forth. I'd meet interesting people, and when Rudy came down I'd be able to introduce him to them. One fellow offered us the use of his apartment in Havana, and we went over and stayed there for a while; then Rudy and I rented a house on Varadero Beach, which I thought was the most beautiful place I'd ever seen. We had a nice little place on the edge of the Du Pont estate, which was being constructed at the time. The tradewinds blew constantly and we didn't need screens on the windows because there weren't any mosquitoes or flies. A husband and wife cooked our food and took care of the house and it was heaven. Cuba was a paradise for rich Americans in those days. In later years, just after Castro had taken over, my father went to Havana with Buck, who was smuggling money out of the country for refugees, and he loved to stand on the corners of the main streets downtown and watch the sexy Cuban women walk by without girdles. That was my father in his old age. Those were nice years, nice trips. Rudy had his dealings with the boys in Havana—Lansky's headquarters, as I remember, were in the Hotel Nacional—but so long as I had my place on Varadero Beach nothing bothered me.

Back in Chicago, however, I began to have serious trouble with Rudy. I was tired of the bums he hung out with and his always having to be at the store. If I had been able to have my own house and not had to live in the hotel things would have been better, but Rudy wouldn't allow it. The glamour of chasing around to different nightclubs and restaurants paled. Rudy was always at the store, treating some showgirl for a boil or a pimple, taking them in the back, girls with nothing on under their mink coats, and giving them a shot of penicillin for the clap or a bad cold. Rudy would take care of everything, everyone loved him around there. He was a marvelous pharmacist and a forceful salesman. Rudy could sell you something white when you wanted black. He was amazing that way. If he could take advantage of someone businesswise, he didn't lose a moment; outside of business though, he'd give you the shirt off his back.

Aside from the drugstore Rudy had a variety of businesses: car agencies with Bruno, interest in a couple of restaurants, a wholesale liquor warehouse. We never had a bank account; Rudy kept his money in safety deposit boxes in the big hotels. Whenever he needed to make a "deposit" he'd have me go over with the cash and put it in the box. There was a different safety deposit box for every dealing: one for the racing book at the Drake, one for the liquor store at the Ambassador, and so on. The money meant nothing to me, I never saw it; I just put it in the vaults. Sometimes Rudy would give me too much cash and I'd have to bring it back to him. "Why didn't you put it in the box?" he'd say, and I'd tell him that I couldn't stuff any more in, it was too full.

I finally convinced Rudy to invest some money in a building on the Near North Side, an apartment house. It was a grand old building with gorgeous flats, and I said, "How long before one of these apartments will be vacant? How long before we can move in?" I was tired of life in the Seneca; it was no place to raise a family, Jimmy was getting older. I didn't like being used by my friends in the hotel who would say to me, "Don't tell Frank that I was out drinking this afternoon with Ralph, okay, honey? Tell him I was with you." That kind of stuff.

Of course it was interesting when someone like Ginger Rogers or Tony Martin came into town. They were friends of Rudy's and I liked to go over to wherever they were staying and have dinner and talk. Ginger Roger's mother was always entertaining for Rudy, she loved him; and Rudy would say to everyone, "Oh you have to meet my beautiful wife." I must admit he was constant, he did love me. I wondered whether or not I really loved him, though. It was the glamour, the high life that I'd been attracted to, but it was now wearing thin.

~

Rudy had an Aunt, Jennie Ashkenaz, who was like a mother to him. Jennie and her husband, Lou, were very well off. Lou had made his money in the beer business, and in their old age their great passion was the racetrack. Jennie used to love to take me with her out to Sportsman's or Arlington or Maywood, wherever the horses were running. She taught me to always look down on the ground at the track in case somebody had dropped some money or a good ticket, and she taught me how to read the *Racing Form*. Jennie was in her sixties then, a tiny, birdlike woman with dyed black hair and a little rosebud mouth full of lipstick. I loved her, we thought alike, and she showed me how to make Jewish dishes. We'd prepare big dinners together for Lou and Rudy in her magnificent Lake Shore Drive apartment that was filled with fine antiques. One time Rudy called up and said he couldn't make it for dinner, he was tied up at the store. I was about to say all right and hang up but Jennie took the phone and yelled at him, telling Rudy to get there as soon as possible if he knew what was good for him. And he came right over! She was full of the devil and a great friend; there wasn't anything anyone could put over on Lou or Jennie.

Jennie made sure that her daughters, all four of them, married millionaires. Her daughter Gloria's husband went to prison for his father, and when he got out he collected a few million bucks. This was before I knew Rudy. Gloria was in love with Rudy and while her husband was in jail they had some kind of affair; they were first cousins. Gloria was beautiful but nutty, and after her husband got out they resumed the marriage. Jennie knew about Gloria's crush on Rudy, in fact she was the one who told me about it, but she never let on to Rudy that she knew, and I never mentioned it to him.

When I married Rudy, Rachel, Jennie and Lou's oldest daughter, who had married into high society in Chicago, threw a dinner party for us. Rudy's family, with the exception of his sister Esther, were all wonderful to me, they wanted to show me off. I was still modeling a little then and of course Rudy always saw to it that I had the most beautiful clothes and hats. I tried my best to get along with Esther, too, but she was very cold and made me feel like I was stealing her brother away from her. Jennie didn't much care for Esther and when Rachel didn't invite her to the dinner party she had for Rudy and me Esther held it against me, and we never did become friends.

Jennie was a good friend, but I was lonely. A fellow named Bob Rawson came to dinner one night with us and the next day he came over to the hotel to see me. He was a gorgeous man, an army major at the time, and he wanted to have an affair with me. I felt like running away with him. He was so handsome that I was tempted, I was just momentarily stricken. I turned him down, I wouldn't sleep with him. And I didn't hide it from Rudy. I told him how lonely I was, how I wanted to move, how tempted I'd been to go off with Bob Rawson. Rudy got angry, of course, and said, "If he comes near here I'll beat him up." Rudy was half Bob Rawson's size but I knew he meant it and I made sure I never saw Rawson again. I had so many opportunities like that, but I didn't like the crowd we were running around with; they were all phonies and hot shots with a lot of money and no sense.

Everything felt wrong to me. I felt that I'd rather be on a tropical island with only my bathing suit, drinking coconut milk and watching my son play in the sand. I wanted to take Jimmy and run away for good. My eczema came back, I started going to different doctors, and finally I had it over my entire body, including my face, where I'd never had it before. I was a mess.

Rudy liked to live hard, to be on the go every minute of the day. He had tremendous energy and had more friends than anyone I've ever known. There's a plaque up in Holy Name Cathedral in Chicago with his name on it, which is a great honor. The bishop used to call Rudy up when he was sick and have him come over to talk with him and show him how to take his medicine. We were friends with the owners of the Club Alabam, a place for all of the visiting firemen and cheating husbands. The club had pretty good food, good entertainment, and the showgirls made a lot of money on the side. We used to go riding at the stables the Alabam owners kept in the country. Rudy was pals with Tony Zale, the boxer, who had a restaurant across the street. One night I walked over to the store and there were Rudy and Tony standing in the street, watching a fellow sweep up broken glass from the sidewalk. I asked what had happened and Tony laughed. "Rudy put another guy through the window," he said. I remembered Eddie Danillo, and asked Rudy why he'd done it. "The guy was giving one of the girls a hard time," Rudy said, meaning one of the showgirls from next door. "She was having a cup of coffee and he wouldn't leave her alone, so I threw him out." "Yeah, only he forgot to open the door first," said Tony.

This kind of thing went on all the time. I was fed up with all of Rudy's hoodlum friends, the so-called celebrities and tough-guy talk. It appealed to me after a drink or two, when I would enjoy the atmosphere; but the next morning I was always sorry to have been part of it, to have allowed these people over to mess up the place. Rudy liked to have people around and have parties, and there was no limit to the booze. He brought up one case of sparkling burgundy after another, that and whatever else anyone wanted.

After a particularly wild party that had lasted into the wee hours of the morning, after all of the people had gone, I looked around at the debris and then at Rudy, who was saying, "Come on, Peg, let's have one more drink." I looked straight at him and said, "You know, I'm going to leave you. I want a divorce." I told him that I was serious, I didn't like this life. Rudy turned pale and said if I left him he would commit suicide. "I'm going to get outside and walk around the sixteenth floor on the side of the building," he said. "If you don't stay with me I'll jump off." It was the alcohol talking, of course, and he didn't go out the window. He cried and put his head in my lap, so I said all right, but that we had to try to make a stab at more down-to-earth living. Rudy cried and cried and said yes, he'd slow down, things would be different, Jimmy and I were all he had. I didn't believe him but he was my husband and I couldn't leave; not yet, anyway.

Soon after this my eczema worsened and infection set in. I told Rudy I had to get away and took Jimmy to my mother's house. I was hospitalized because I was running a fever and my skin was blistered from head to toe. The doctors called it neurodermatitis and I was swathed in bandages. My skin would stick to the bandages and when they were unwound I'd scream. The doctors admitted they didn't know what to do with me, they were experimenting.

I was given an oil bath everyday, in order to loosen the bandages, and put under a heat lamp. Medical students were brought in to see me, the worst case of dermatitis they'd ever had. I looked like the Mummy. Rudy's brother Bruno didn't believe that I was as sick as I was; he told Rudy he thought I was faking, I was acting, it couldn't be that bad. Rudy brought him to the hospital and he was horrified; I smelled so badly from the open sores that Bruno couldn't take it, he had to leave.

I was in a private room, and Rudy made sure that I was given the best care. I remember during this time thinking perhaps I never would get better, that I'd always have to be wrapped up, hidden. One of my favorite films from around that time was *Pepe Le Moko*, with Jean Gabin starring as a Parisian gangster hiding out in Algiers, and I imagined myself living the rest of my life covered up like an Arab woman, sequestered in the Kasbah.

After two months in the hospital my condition began to improve. My face cleared up first and one day the doctor walked in and said, "My, what a pretty young girl." He'd never been able to see my face before. Amazingly, I didn't have a scar. The doctors suggested to Rudy that he take me away on a long trip, take me someplace where I wouldn't have any aggravation and could recover my health. So Rudy made arrangements for Jimmy to stay at my parents' house and we left for Hawaii.

Rudy thought that he could do some business in the islands—I guess the boys were opening up some operations out there—and I was glad to get out of the hospital. A girlfriend of mine, Arlene Carrol, who'd been a high-fashion model in Chicago and New York, and had been a *Vanity Fair* cover girl, had married a doctor from Honolulu and with him had opened up one of the swankiest resort hotels in Hawaii. Rudy and I rented one of their cottages and Arlene saw to it that I had everything I needed. It must have been very expensive but Rudy didn't care. Nothing was too good for his wife.

I spent six months in Hawaii, living in a bathing suit with no makeup, only an orchid in my hair. Rudy was back and forth between Honolulu and Chicago, and through his business associates and Arlene Carrol we met some wonderful people, most of whom were Chinese. We went to the Chinese theater, and to the Kabuki, marvelous outdoor restaurants, and had the best time of our lives. Rudy made a few very successful contacts and established a racing book and gambling casino, so he was happy. I regained my health and felt and looked like a million dollars.

As soon as we got back to Chicago, however, I began to get nervous again. The same old lifestyle resumed and I knew that if I didn't make a change I'd break down in the same way, only worse. This time when I told Rudy I was leaving he didn't argue with me. He was very unhappy about it but said all right, let's try it living apart for a while. We decided to separate, not divorce immediately, and see what happened. I went to my mother's with Jimmy; she was glad to have me living at home, and I went out with Rudy at night.

Jennie Ashkenaz begged me to give Rudy another chance; she desperately wanted to keep me in the family. She promised that I would have money, jewelry, whatever I wanted, but I couldn't do it, I rebelled. I didn't want to be the "playgirl" anymore, the pretty girl always on display. I didn't have anything of my own, not really. I was continually put down by Rudy and he was incapable of understanding how I felt. He loved me, that was true, he promised me the moon, but he couldn't see the problem. My mother kept after me to divorce Rudy, to make another, cleaner life for myself; so I did, I got a divorce. Rudy bought off my attorney—the guy I'd met in Las Vegas a couple of years or so before—and I was awarded twenty-five dollars a week for Jimmy, that's all. Rudy paid for the attorney.

I didn't care about not getting a large settlement, I was free. I thought to myself, now my troubles are over; but they were only just beginning.

~

My mother was too sick to look after Jimmy all of the time, and I couldn't afford to have Flo or another girl around, so I stayed home. It was difficult, though, because I didn't want to place the entire financial burden on my father. Through an old girlfriend of my brother's I got a job working at the Furniture Mart on Fridays. I was called a Friday Girl and showed customers the line and made cocktails at four o'clock. It was very easy, all I had to do was look nice and be sharp with the customers, the buyers, be able to talk intelligently and keep them happy. It wasn't much of a job but I did make a little money and contacts with the various wholesalers in case I wanted anything at cost.

The buyers would bring me presents, silk stockings, flowers, boxes of chocolates, and ask me out; but I didn't want to date. The other girls would say that I was being silly, that I should take advantage of the situation and begin dating again. I had had it with the high life, I didn't want it anymore. I didn't want to run out and smoke and drink. In fact, I had given up smoking, mainly because I lost too many gold cigarette cases and I thought it was a waste of money. Rudy and I would go into El Morocco and I'd leave the case on the table. I'd want to go back to get it but he'd just say, "Leave it, don't worry. I'll buy you another one." Rudy was crazy that way, he had a strange attitude about things, especially where I was concerned. He wanted complete control over me and I was loath to become involved with another man who might try to do the same thing.

After a while, after more prodding by the girls at work and encouragement from my mother, I began to go out on dates. I made great demands of my suitors, however. I expected them to bring me gifts of the finest French perfume on the first date, to come to the door with flowers for my mother. This is what I had learned to expect, and if they didn't do it I didn't have to go out with them. I really was longing for a nice boy, to have a little house of my own, more children; this is how I felt. But men were always putting me in a different role: they would take me out and buy me beautiful things and put me on a pedestal, the beautiful princess. I wanted these nice things, I was used to them, but at the same time I wanted to settle down in a modest way. I was confused, mixed up; I knew and I didn't know. To what standards should I conform? I was secretly battling with my desire to call my old boyfriend Hal French, but my ego, my pride, wouldn't permit me to do it. I don't know that Hal would have been the answer to my confusion but I never allowed myself to find out.

I'd drive by the middle- and upper-middle-class homes with lights on in the windows and I'd picture the mother in the kitchen, the father sitting in the living room reading his paper and smoking his pipe—like a frame from a Frank Capra film, *It's a Wonderful Life*—that kind of sentimental, homey scene. It frustrated me to think about it, because Rudy and I had certainly had the money to live that way, and I couldn't have it. I was very upset about this for a very long time, and I blamed Rudy, rightly or wrongly, for preventing me from establishing this kind of idealized lifestyle.

My mother was doing what she could with Jimmy but she began, finally, to throw up to me the fact that I left him with her so much. She didn't feel it was good for her health, that it was putting an undue hardship on her. She was right, I knew this, and I felt guilty about it. Years later I felt that I had unnecessarily contributed to the premature death of my mother, that I had given her too much work to do, had burdened her with the care of my son.

When Rudy and I had gotten divorced the photographers had come to the court and, foolishly, I'd let them take my picture while I was sitting on the top of a desk with my legs crossed. The next day in the newspaper they blew the case out of proportion, running a photo of me with a big smile and my skirt hiked up under the headline "Chicago Debutante Divorces Playboy." The story said that Rudy had one hundred suits and two hundred ties in his closet, quoting him to the effect that he'd rather live in the closet than with me, that kind of nonsense. I didn't think much about it at the time, I laughed it off, but for months afterward I received crank calls. This, too, upset my mother.

Not long after the divorce my mother and I were sitting and talking and she reminded me of an incident that occurred when I was seventeen years old. She and I had been walking downtown in the Loop, the streets were very crowded, and a man came up to us holding a camera. He asked my mother, while he was looking at me, if he could take my picture. He said there was a contest where Dorothy Lamour was going to choose a girl to have a screen test, and the contest photographers were stopping girls on the street, wherever they spotted an attractive young lady, and photographing them. The finalists were to be invited to the Chicago Theater on State Street for the judging. We allowed him to go ahead and take my picture and a few days later I received a call asking me to come down to the theater. There was a group photo taken in the lobby of the theater, which I was in, but then I got so shy that I made some excuse about having to go to the rest room and instead of going up on stage with the other girls, I ran out the door.

"You were such a good girl, Peggy," said my mother as she recalled the incident. "You were so shy and afraid to offend anyone. I thought everything would be so wonderful for you, so easy." I knew she was disappointed with what I'd done with my life so far, and I was determined to change direction. I just wasn't sure how to go about it.

Coda:
The Mystery

Coda: *The Mystery*

If my father were alive today he would be eighty-six years old. A few years ago, my son, Asa, and I visited his grave in Chicago for the first time. He's buried in a different cemetery than his father, in a plot owned by his sister and brother-in-law, on the far west side of the city. A female clerk in the cemetery office, while researching the location of the grave, told us that his site had been moved, but she would not tell us when or why, since I could not prove that I was a member of the family. She did, however, give us a printed map of the cemetery and marked the route to the grave.

We found his stone easily. I was immediately surprised that the year of my father's birth engraved on the marble slab was one year earlier than I had understood it to be. Also, I had never known his precise birth date before—August thirteenth. Neither of his wives could remember it. When I asked my mother she told me, "I think maybe in September, possibly August. It was a warm month."

I realized long ago that if forced to choose between revelation and mystery, I'll take mystery every time. Revelations solve very little; they serve only to preclude further thought, whereas mysteries continue to force speculation. The object, I concluded, is to encourage invention, not reduce possibilities.

My son and I stood there, thirty-five years after my father's death, on a midsummer's day, and I thought of Blind Lemon Jefferson's lyric: "If there's one kind favor I'd ask of you, it's to see that my grave is kept clean." At least now we knew exactly when he'd been born. I picked up two small stones, handed one to Asa, and told him to kiss it and place it on top of the headstone, which he did. This was a Jewish custom, I said, although I don't know how or from what occasion I could have remembered it.

"I wish you could have met your grandchildren, Dad," I said. I kissed my stone and placed it next to my son's. "And I wish you could have met me, too."

THE FOLLOWING IS THE CRIMINAL RECORD OF RUDOLPH A. WINSTON, FBI #322954:

Contributor of Fingerprints	Name & No.	Arrested or Charge Rcvd.	Disposition
Prob. Unit, Chicago, Ill.	Rudolph Aaron Winston, #___	8-10-32	Violation of N.P.A.
U.S. Marshal Chicago, Ill.	Rudolph Aaron Winston, #___	8-11-32	N.P.A.
PD, Chicago, Ill., Prob.	Rudolph Winston #D-22959	3-17-42	R.S.P. 1 Yr.
BFD, Chicago, Ill.	Rudolph Aaron Winston, #99–799	Inquiry 1-16-45	

About the Author

Barry Gifford's books have been translated in twenty-two languages. His recent books include *Wyoming*, a novel; *Out of the Past*, essays on films; and *Replies to Wang Wei*, a collection of poems.

Barry Gifford lives in the San Francisco Bay area and can be found at www.barrygifford.com.